it girl knits

it girl knits

phoenix bess

30 Fresh Styles for the Young and Fabulous

POTTER
CRAFT

NEW YORK

This book is dedicated to my family.

Published in the United States by Potter Craft, an imprint of the
Crown Publishing Group, a division of Random House, Inc., New York.
www.pottercraft.com

POTTER CRAFT and colophon is a registered trademark of
Random House, Inc.

Library of Congress Cataloging-in-Publication Data is available
upon request.

ISBN: 978-0-307-39634-1
Printed in China

Design by Jennifer K. Beal Davis
Photographs by Dan Howell
Illustrations by Elizabeth Sullivan

Thanks to the Craft Yarn Council of America (www.yarnstandards.com) for
their Standard Yarn Weights System Chart, which appears on page 137.

10 9 8 7 6 5 4 3 2 1

First Edition

acknowledgments

Many people helped make this book happen, and I have to thank them.

Elizabeth Sullivan, you're totally awesome. Thanks for turning my designs into items that someone else can actually make. Peggy Greig, thanks for technically editing Elizabeth's patterns with so much attention to detail and for rescuing errant packages. Nicky Epstein, I've loved your books ever since I started knitting. Thanks for your support and book publishing advice and for introducing me to my editor. Kirk Schroder, thanks for taking care of all the legal stuff; you rock! Thanks to my wonderful knitters, crafters, and seamstresses: Diane Hoegerl, Marianne Henderson, Polli Romey, Suzie Layton, Judy Lewis, Dee Smith, Allie Mathis, Donna Mathis, Debbie Sullivan, and Margaret Sullivan. Thank you to Rosy Ngo, Melissa Bonventre, Courtney Conroy, Chi Ling Moy, Jennifer K. Beal Davis, Kristen Petliski, Dan Howell, and the entire team at Potter Craft for helping me make this book.

Thank you to all the folks in my community who have encouraged and supported me. Miss Rosalie, thanks for teaching me to knit. Maggie, thank you for your unfailing support. And Dia and Ned, thanks for always making Southwind a welcoming place to design. Candy, Mary, and Nancy, thanks for letting me meet with my knitters at The Bay Window and for all your support. Mathews Post Office ladies, thank you for your patience and helpfulness with my have-to-get-there-tomorrow packages to knitters across the United States and Canada.

I send a special thank you to all of my family and friends for their encouragement and support through the years. Aunt Elaine, thanks for being the classiest lady I know—your style is awesome. Austin, thanks for being my chauffeur, chef, confidante, and friend through all of this craziness. Blake, thanks for making my website, marketing materials, and beautiful photographs for so many years. Dad, thanks for tons of encouragement. Most importantly, thanks, Mom for being the best mom I could ask for and for making this book happen.

contents

introduction

Put simply, I design what I would wear. I begin with clean, classic lines, then look for ways to add a fun, flirty edginess. I'm often drawn to conflicting elements that don't seem to match. For me, a rough earthy look can be as inspiring as polished New York high fashion. Sometimes mixing the two makes the best design; it's something that just kind of happens.

One of the ways I add interest to my garments is with fun embellishments. I think that handwork, sewing, and crafting is an expression of personality and individuality. I've been beading, making jewelry, and sewing clothes for as long as I can remember, and for me, knitting is a natural extension of these skills.

I prefer to use natural fibers when I design. Natural fibers are the key to high-quality garments that drape and fit well. For the projects in this book, I chose from an array of bamboo, silk, and cotton yarns. To find just the right yarns, I spent months swatching countless skeins to match them to the qualities that each garment needed. I'm really picky about softness, so I made sure that all of the yarns feel comfortable. I also took special care to make sure that the garments are as easy to care for as they are fun to wear.

Almost every project in this book is knitted in the round. That means less seaming, finishing, and purling to slow you down. I've always designed my garments with circular construction, and even though they have a sophisticated cut and drape, they are actually quite easy to make. It's important to me that girls of all sizes are able to enjoy wearing these designs, so many of the patterns include instructions for adding length to hemlines, inseams, and waistlines. Girls with curves are represented, too, with customizable shaping across the seat of each pants pattern. While all of this may sound complicated, it's not. Most of the projects are suitable for beginners, with instructions that are easy to follow.

I hope you enjoy making, embellishing, and wearing these garments as much as I enjoyed designing them for you.

Cheers,

Phoenix

it girl style guide

Your knitted wardrobe needs to be versatile so you can make a million cute combinations for every occasion. This book is divided into four sections, each focusing on a different activity in your life: relaxing, recreating, and celebrating. The sections feature garments and accessories perfect for those occasions, with styles, fabrics, and colors that suit each activity.

To show you how to coordinate yarn colors, mix and match garment styles, and add optional designer details to best showcase your new garment, each pattern includes a tip called "It Girl Style Secrets." These tips will teach you how to look your absolute best.

Be sure to reference the handy chart below for color-matching tips. Its position at the front of the book makes it easy to flip to when you're planning your projects. Seek advice from your local yarn store owner when selecting yarns for your projects.

it girl color matches

Lavender + Baby Pink = cuteness

Hot Pink + Lime Green = very Lily Pullitzer

Black + Anything = duh

Medium Blue + Seafoam Green = breezy

White + Anything = double duh

Purple + Pink = pretty

Turquoise + Pink = fresh

it girl
patterns

sunny
days

It's a sunny afternoon of shopping and hanging out with your favorite people. What are you wearing in this picture? You could be wearing completely unique no-one-else-has-one-like-it garments. When you're wearing your own stylish clothes, every day is a good day. Sure, you're working hard at everything you do, but you can look great while you do it. Knit up a cute top and matching pants or a skirt in colors that suit your personality and style. Whether your day is spent on a campus or at the mall, your look will rock.

baby doll top

Skill Level

Intermediate

Size

XS (S, M, L, XL)

Finished Measurements

Empire Waist Circumference (just under the bust): 24 (26, 30, 34, 36)" (61 [66, 76, 86, 91]cm)
Length (excluding straps): 19 (20, 21¼, 22½, 23¾)" (48.5, 51, 54, 57, 60.5]cm)

Yarn

▦ 7 (8, 9, 10, 11) skeins Needful Yarns Dubai Stretch, 85% viscose, 15% Elite PBT, 1¾ oz (50g), 182 yd (166m), #109 Lime Green, **3** light

Needles and Notions

▦ US size 7 (4.5mm) circular needle, 24" (61cm) long, or size needed to obtain gauge
▦ US size F-5 (3.75mm) crochet hook
▦ Stitch markers
▦ Yarn needle
▦ Sewing needle and lime green thread
▦ 1 yd (1m) grosgrain ribbon, 1½" (4cm) wide, lime green
▦ 1 yd (1m) satin ribbon, ⅜" (10mm) wide, lime green
▦ 2 yd (2m) M&J Trimming Hand-dyed Silk Satin Ribbon, 1½" (4cm) wide, #25179 Fresh Celery

Gauge

26 stitches and 40 rounds = 4" (10cm) in stockinette stitch when worked in the round, after washing.
Adjust needle size as necessary to obtain correct gauge.

Soft and feminine, this little top will be a versatile part of your knitted wardrobe. Dress it up with a skirt for a night out, or dress it down with jeans for a quick trip to the mall. Worked mostly in the round for easy construction, details like the pretty silk ribbon sash make it look anything but simple. The yarn is stretchy and soft, and you'll reach for this top again and again.

Notes

1. The yarn shrinks by 10% when washed according to manufacturer's suggested method. Check gauge on a washed swatch.
2. The Left Cup and the Right Cup are worked flat (back and forth in rows) in separate pieces.
3. The Back Inset is worked separately, back and forth in rows. Stitches are added for the front, and the Body is worked in the round from the bust to the hem.

Left Cup

Cast on 66 (72, 78, 86, 94) stitches. Purl 1 row.

Shape Neck Edge

Row 1 (RS) Knit to last 4 stitches, k2tog, k2.
Row 2 Purl.

Repeat these 2 rows 13 (13, 13, 15, 15) times more—52 (58, 64, 70, 78) stitches remain.

Shape Side Edge

Row 1 (RS) K2, ssk, knit to last 4 stitches, k2tog, k2.
Row 2 Purl.

Repeat these 2 rows 22 (25, 28, 31, 35) more times—6 stitches remain.

Next Row K2, k2tog, k2.

Purl 1 row.

Next Row K1, slip 2 stitches, k1, p2sso, k1, binding off all stitches at the same time.

Right Cup

Cast on 66 (72, 78, 86, 94) stitches. Purl 1 row.

Shape Neck Edge
Row 1 (RS) K2, ssk, knit to end.
Row 2 Purl.

Repeat these 2 rows 13 (13, 15, 15, 15) times more—52 (58, 64, 70, 78) stitches remain.

Shape Side Edge
Row 1 (RS) K2, ssk, knit to last 4 stitches, k2tog, k2.
Row 2 Purl.

Repeat these 2 rows 22 (25, 28, 31, 35) times more—6 stitches remain.

Next Row K2, k2tog, k2.

Purl 1 row.

Next Row K1, slip 2 stitches, k1, p2sso, k1, binding off all stitches at the same time.

Body

Back Inset
Cast on 78 (84, 98, 111, 117) stitches. Work back and forth in stockinette stitch for 3 (3, 3, 3¼, 3¼)" (7.5 [7.5, 7.5, 8, 8]cm).

If you're not already working on circular needles, slip stitches onto circulars, and cast on 78 (84, 98, 111, 117) stitches at the beginning of the row. Place marker, and join for working in the round, being careful not to twist stitches—156 (168, 196, 222, 234) stitches total.

Waist Sash

Work even in stockinette stitch for 1¾" (4.5cm).

Increase Round Beginning at marker, *k12 (12, 14, 16, 16), k1f&b in next 54 (60, 70, 79, 85) stitches, k12 (12, 14, 16, 16); repeat from * to end once—264 (288, 336, 380, 404) stitches total.

Work even in stockinette stitch until the piece measures 14½ (15, 15½, 16, 16½)" (37 [38, 39.5, 40.5, 42]cm) from beginning of sash. Bind off.

Finishing

Place pins 3" (7.5cm) in from both sides of the Left Cup. Sew a running stitch to gather the material between the pins to measure 1½ (2, 3, 4, 4½)" (4 [5, 7.5, 10, 11.5]cm). The Left Cup should measure 7½ (8, 9, 10, 10½)" (19 [20.5, 23, 25.5, 26.5]cm) at the bottom edge. Fasten on the wrong side to secure the gathers. Repeat to gather the Right Cup.

Sew the sides of the Back Inset to the sides of each cup. Sew the cast-on edge of the Body halfway across the cast-on edges of the cups on both sides, ensuring that the rows line up properly. The center of the Body and cups are unsewn. Try on the garment to check fit. Continue seaming across Left Cup first. The Right Cup will overlap the left by approximately 3" (7.5cm) at the center of the body. Continue sewing across the Right Cup, working 1 row below the Left Cup where the cups overlap.

With right side facing, join yarn and single crochet around the sides of each cup. Weave in ends. Hand wash in warm water with mild detergent. Wring and blot to remove excess water, and dry flat.

····· it girl style secret

The Baby Doll Top is meant to be sweet and flirty. Slim bottoms offset its billowy looseness, so pair it with the Comfy Cotton Pants (page 41), slim jeans, or cutoff shorts.

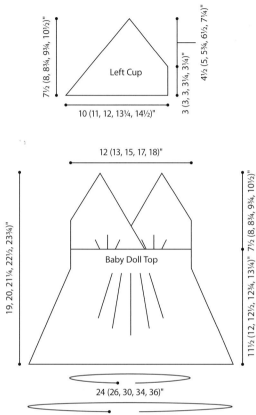

Left Cup

7½ (8, 8¾, 9¾, 10½)"

4½ (5, 5¾, 6½, 7¼)"

10 (11, 12, 13¼, 14½)"

3 (3, 3¼, 3¼)"

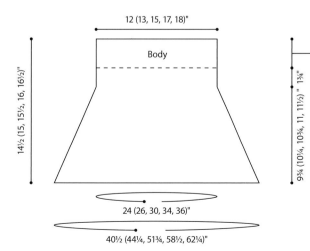

12 (13, 15, 17, 18)"

Baby Doll Top

19, 20, 21¼, 22½, 23¾)"

11½ (12, 12½, 12¾, 13¼)" 7½ (8, 8¾, 9¾, 10½)"

24 (26, 30, 34, 36)"

40½ (44¼, 51¾, 58½, 62¼)"

12 (13, 15, 17, 18)"

Body

14½ (15, 15½, 16, 16½)"

9¾ (10¼, 10¾, 11, 11½)" 1¾"

3 (3, 3, 3¼, 3¼)"

24 (26, 30, 34, 36)"

40½ (44¼, 51¾, 58½, 62¼)"

Straps

Cut 2 lengths of the narrow ⅜" satin ribbon 15" (38cm) long. Fold over the ends of each ribbon by ½ (13mm), and sew together to form a double thickness. Tack 1 end of 1 ribbon to the wrong side of the top point of the Left Cup. Repeat on the Right Cup with the other ribbon. Try on the top to determine the correct strap length. Pin ribbons to the wrong side of the back, 3¾–4" (9–10cm) in from the side seams. With sewing needle and matching thread, tack straps in place on wrong side of garment.

Ribbon Belt

Cut a 15 (16, 18, 20, 21)" (38 [40.5, 45.5, 51, 53.5]cm) length of the 1½" (4cm) grosgrain ribbon (length equal to the width of the front of the knitted sash to the side seams when worn).

Cut the length of ribbon in half, and with an iron set on silk setting, press out any wrinkles. Lay the 2 lengths over grosgrain, overlapping the long edges slightly and allowing the excess at each short ends to extend equally at both edges of grosgrain. Tack in place carefully with matching thread.

Try on the garment, and pin the ribbon belt to the front of the knitted sash. Take off garment and carefully tack ribbon belt in place with a loose running stitch along each end and in 2 places at the top edge of the sash, under the cups.

beaded
bandana

Skill Level

Intermediate

Size

One size

Finished Measurements

Width: 30" (76cm)
Length: 11¾" (30cm)

Yarn

▨ 1 skein Tilli Tomas Fil de la Mer, 60%
silk, 40% seacell, 1¾ oz (50g), 140 yd
(128m), Mermaid, ⓸ medium

Needles and Notions

▨ 40g package Dyna-Mites™ Seed
Bead, #6, Inside Color Lilac
▨ 40g package Dyna-Mites™ Seed
Bead, #6, Frosted Transparent AB Teal
▨ Medium steel beading needle
▨ US size 7 (4.5mm) knitting needles, or
size needed to obtain gauge
▨ Yarn needle
▨ Aleene's® Fabric Fusion™ Permanent
Dry Cleanable Fabric Adhesive™

Gauge

16 stitches and 24 rows = 4" (10cm) in
Fishnet Lace Pattern (at right) when
worked flat.
Adjust needle size as necessary to obtain
correct gauge.

Notes

1. Beads are threaded onto the working
yarn with a beading needle before
beginning to knit. Alternate the bead
colors when threading on the yarn, as
instructed in the pattern.

I like small one-skein projects that are colorful
and unique. So, I worked out an easy beginner
lace stitch to showcase this amazing variegated
yarn made from silk and seaweed. Knitting with
beads is easy, and they look like sea glass
scattered on ocean waves.

2. Slip 1 bead in place from the working yarn on each
yarn over (yo) of the fishnet lace pattern.
3. The Bandana is knit sideways, from side point to
side point. Stitches are increased every other row to
the full width at the center point, then decreased to
the end.

Abbreviations

K1f&b: Knit into the front of the next stitch as usual,
but leave that stitch on the left-hand needle and knit
into the back loop of the same stitch. Then, slide the
stitch off of the left-hand needle—1 stitch increased.
Psso: Pass slipped stitch over.

Bandana

Using the steel beading needle, thread about 50
seed beads onto the working yarn, alternating colors.

Shape Right Half
Cast on 1 stitch.
Row 1 K1f&b—2 stitches.
Row 2 (RS) K1, yo (slip a bead from yarn into place on
this and every yo), k1—3 stitches.
Row 3 K1, yo, k2—4 stitches.
Row 4 Knit.
Row 5 K1, yo, k2tog, yo, k1—5 stitches.
Row 6 Knit.
Row 7 K1, yo, k2tog, yo, k2—6 stitches.
Row 8 Knit.
Row 9 K1, yo, k2tog, yo, k2tog, yo, k1—7 stitches.
Row 10 Knit.
Row 11 K1, *yo, k2tog; repeat from * to last 2
stitches, yo, k2—8 stitches.

Row 12 Knit.

Row 13 K1, *yo, k2tog; repeat from * to last stitch, yo, k1—9 stitches.

Row 14 Knit.

Rows 15–90 Repeat rows 11–14, increasing 1 stitch every right-side row—47 stitches after the last row.

Shape Left Half

Row 91 K1, yo, slip 1, k2tog, psso, *yo, k2tog; repeat from * to last stitch, yo, k1-47 stitches.

Row 92 Knit to last 4 stitches, k2tog, k2—46 stitches.

Row 93 K1, yo, slip 1, k2tog, psso, *yo, k2tog; repeat from * to last 2 stitches, yo, k2—46 stitches.

Row 94 Knit to last 4 stitches, k2tog, k2—45 stitches.

Rows 95–170 Repeat Rows 91–94, decreasing 1 stitch every wrong-side row—7 stitches after the last row.

Row 171 K1, yo, slip 1, k2tog, psso, yo, k2tog, yo, k1—7 stitches.

Row 172 K3, k2tog, k2—6 stitches.

Row 173 K1, yo, slip 1, k2tog, psso, yo, k2—6 stitches.

Row 174 K2, k2tog, k2—5 stitches.

Row 175 K1, yo, slip 1, k2tog, psso, yo, k1—5 stitches.

Row 176 K1, k2tog, k2—4 stitches.

Row 177 K1, yo, slip 1, k2tog, psso—3 stitches.

Row 178 K1, k2tog—2 stitches.

Row 179 Slip 1, k1, psso—1 stitch.

Break yarn, and pull yarn through the last stitch to fasten it off.

Finishing

Using yarn needle, weave in ends. Dab Fabric Fusion™ or clear fabric glue on any ends that won't stay tucked in. To block, spritz the Beaded Bandana with cool water until damp, and lay flat on a piece of foam board or carpet. Gently pull all the edges into a triangle shape and pin them to hold the shape while drying.

knitting with beads

1. Refer to pattern instructions for the number of beads needed.
2. Thread the eye of the beading needle with the pattern yarn.
3. Pick up beads, following instructions for the order in which to place beads on the yarn, and slide them onto the needle and yarn.
4. Follow pattern instructions for casting on and the set-up rows.
5. To place a bead, insert the right-hand needle into the stitch on the left-hand needle as usual, but before bringing the working yarn around to form the next stitch, slide the bead to the base of the previous stitch, flush with the right-hand needle.
6. Bring the working yarn around, and slide the stitch off the left-hand needle.
7. Continue knitting, sliding each bead tightly against the right-hand needle each time to ensure that the bead will appear on the front of the work.

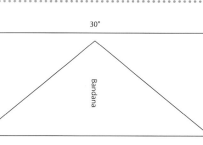

30"

Bandana

11¾"

it girl style secret

Wear your bandana with anything!

flirty short
skirt

Skill Level

Easy

Sizes

XS (S, M, L, XL)

Finished Measurements

Waist: 25 (27, 31, 35, 37)" (63.5 [68.5, 79, 89, 94]cm)
Length: 17½ (17½, 18, 18½, 18½)" (44.5 [44.5, 45.5, 47, 47]cm)

Yarn

▦ 3 (4, 4, 4, 5) skeins Southwest Trading Company Bamboo, 100% bamboo, 3½ oz (100g), 250 yd (229m), #402 Magenta, (**3**) light

Needles and Notions

▦ US size 5 (3.75mm) circular needle, 24" (61cm) long, or size needed to obtain gauge
▦ US size F-5 (3.75mm) crochet hook
▦ Stitch markers
▦ Yarn needle
▦ 1 yd (91cm) waistband elastic, ½" (13mm) wide
▦ Sewing needle and thread

Gauge

24 stitches and 36 rounds = 4" (10cm) in stockinette stitch when worked in the round. Adjust needle size as necessary to obtain correct gauge.

Notes

1. The skirt is worked in the round in 1 piece from the hem to the waist.
2. The hem is divided into 6 sections with stitch markers.

Made with an amazing 100% bamboo yarn that feels like pure silk, this handkerchief-hem skirt is designed to match the Lacy Camisole (page 74) perfectly. I love the way that this skirt falls from the hips, rippling slightly, the pretty handkerchief points swirling around your legs as you walk. The skirt is worked in the round, and simple shaping makes the hem points pop.

Skirt

Cast on 462 (474, 498, 522, 534) stitches. Join for working in the round, being careful not to twist stitches.

Set-up Round *Place marker, knit 77 (79, 83, 87, 89) stitches; repeat from * to end 5 more times.

Round 1 Knit.
Round 2 *Ssk, knit to 3 stitches before next marker, k2tog, k1; repeat from * to end of round.

Repeat these 2 rounds 16 more times until 43 (45, 49, 53, 55) stitches remain in each section between markers—258 (270, 294, 318, 330) stitches total.

Rounds 1–11 Knit.
Round 12 *Ssk, knit to 3 stitches before next marker, k2tog, k1; repeat from * to end of round.

Repeat these 12 rounds 7 more times until 27 (29, 33, 37, 39) stitches remain in each section between markers—162 (174, 198, 222, 234) stitches total.

Rounds 1–3 Knit.
Round 4 *Ssk, knit to 3 stitches before next marker, k2tog, k1; repeat from * to end of round—25 (27, 31, 35, 37) stitches remain in each section between markers—150 (162, 186, 210, 222) stitches total.

Work even in stockinette stitch until skirt measures 17½ (17½, 18, 18½, 18½)" (44.5 [44.5, 45.5, 47, 47]cm) from the cast-on edge. Purl 1 round to create a turning ridge. Work even in stockinette stitch for ¾" (2cm). Bind off.

Finishing

Fold the waistband to the wrong side of the skirt at the turning ridge. Using a yarn needle and matching yarn, whipstitch the bound-off edge to the wrong side, leaving an opening large enough to slide in the waistband elastic; do not break yarn. Cut the elastic 1" (2.5cm) longer than your waist measurement. Feed the elastic through the casing, pulling out both ends. Overlap the elastic ends by 1" (2.5cm), and sew them together with a sewing needle and thread. Slide the elastic back into the casing, and sew the casing closed with the yarn needle and yarn.

Crochet Trim

Round 1 Single crochet in each stitch around bottom edge of skirt.
Round 2 *Single crochet in each of next 4 single crochet, chain 3, slip stitch in same single crochet as last single crochet worked; repeat from * to end. Fasten off.

Weave in ends. Hand wash skirt. Dry flat.

it girl style secret

Wear this skirt with sandals, kitten-heel slides, or ballet flats. Pair it with the matching Lacy Camisole (page 74) to create the perfect outfit for any occasion.

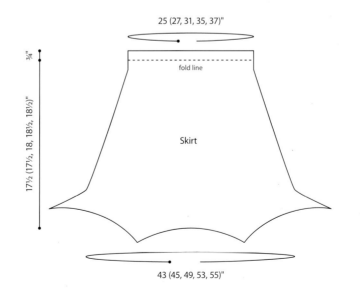

25 (27, 31, 35, 37)"

¾"

fold line

17½ (17½, 18, 18½, 18½)"

Skirt

43 (45, 49, 53, 55)"

shortie
jacket

Skill Level

Intermediate

Sizes

XS (S, M, L, XL)

Finished Measurements

Bust Circumference: 30 (32, 36, 40, 42)"
(76 [81, 91, 101.5, 106.5]cm)
Length: 12 (12, 13, 14, 15)" (30.5 [30.5, 33, 35.5, 38]cm)

Yarn

▦ 7 (8, 9, 10, 11) skeins Berroco Suede, 100% nylon, 1¾ oz (50g), 120 yd (111m), #3727 Dale Evans White, (4️⃣) medium

Needles and Notions

▦ US size 7 (4.5mm) circular needle, 32" (81 cm) long, or size needed to obtain gauge
▦ US size 7 (4.5mm) double-pointed needles, or size needed to obtain gauge
▦ Stitch holders
▦ Stitch marker
▦ Yarn needle

Gauge

20 stitches and 30 rows = 4" (10cm) in stockinette stitch. Adjust needle size as necessary to obtain correct gauge.

Notes

1. The jacket is worked in 1 piece from hem to shoulders. Shoulder seams are then joined, and sleeve stitches are picked up around the armhole. Sleeves are worked in the round from the shoulder down to the cuff.

This versatile jacket is crisp and tiny, and you can wear it with ANYTHING. The timeless one-piece construction and sleeves worked in the round make it so easy to knit, while the soft faux suede yarn provides the perfect hand for couture detailing like a mandarin collar and sleek turned hems.

Body

With the circular needle, cast on 150 (160, 180, 200, 210) stitches. Working back and forth in rows, work 7 rows in stockinette stitch, ending with a right side facing. Knit 1 row on the wrong side to create a turning ridge for the hem.

Cast on 5 stitches at the beginning of the next 2 rows for the front facings—160 (170, 190, 210, 220) stitches total.

To make turning ridges for the facings, work the next 2 rows throughout jacket.

Row 1 (RS) K5, slip 1, knit to last 6 stitches, slip 1, k5.
Row 2 Purl.

Keeping facings as established, continue in stockinette stitch for 5½ (5½, 6, 6½, 7½)" (14 [14, 15, 16.5, 19]cm) from turning ridge, ending with a wrong-side row.

Divide for Armholes

Continuing in pattern as established, work 38 (40, 45, 49, 51) stitches and slip these stitches to a stitch holder for the Right Front, work 9 (10, 10, 12, 13) stitches and slip to a stitch holder for the armhole, work 66 (70, 80, 88, 92) stitches and slip to a stitch holder for Back, work 9 (10, 10, 12, 13) stitches and slip these stitches to a stitch holder for armhole, work 38 (40, 45, 49, 51) stitches for Left Front.

···· it girl style secret

Wear the Shortie Jacket with the Lacy Camisole
(page 74) underneath for a layered look, or create
a sophisticated yet casual look by wearing it with a
tiny tee and jeans.

Left Front

Keeping facing as established, continue in
stockinette stitch on 38 (40, 45, 49, 51) stitches
for Left Front only.

Shape Armhole

Row 1 Purl.
Row 2 K1, ssk, work to end.

Repeat these 2 rows twice more until 35 (37,
42, 46, 48) stitches remain.

Work until the piece measures 2 (2, 2½, 3, 3)"
(5 [5, 6.5, 7.5, 7.5]cm) from the beginning of the
armhole shaping, ending with a wrong-side row.

Purl 1 row on the right side. Work for 2½"
(6.5cm) more, ending with a right-side row.

Shape Neck

Bind off 12 (13, 14, 15, 15) stitches at the
beginning of the next wrong-side row—23 (24,
28, 31, 33) stitches remain.

Row 1 (RS) Knit to last 3 stitches, k2tog, k1.
Rows 2–4 Work even in stockinette stitch.

Repeat these 4 rows 3 more times—19 (20, 24,
27, 29) stitches.

Place stitches on a stitch holder for shoulders.

Right Front

With wrong side facing, slip the 38 (40, 45, 49,
51) stitches from the Right Front stitch holder to
needle. Join yarn, and continue in stockinette
stitch, keeping facing as established.

Shape Armhole

Row 1 Purl.
Row 2 Work in pattern to last 3 stitches, k2tog,
k1.

Repeat these 2 rows twice more—35 (37, 42,
46, 48) stitches.

Work even until piece measures 2 (2, 2½, 3, 3)"
(5 [5, 6.5, 7.5, 7.5]cm) from the beginning of
armhole shaping, ending with a wrong-side row.

Purl 1 row on the right side. Work even for 2½"
(6.5cm) more, ending with a wrong-side row.

Shape Neck

Bind off 12 (13, 14, 15, 15) stitches at the
beginning of the next right-side row—23 (24,
28, 31, 33) stitches.

Row 1 (RS) K1, ssk, work in pattern to end.
Rows 2–4 Work even in stockinette stitch.

Repeat these 4 rows 3 more times—19 (20, 24,
27, 29) stitches.

Place stitches on a stitch holder for shoulders.

Back

With wrong side facing, slip the 66 (70, 80, 88,
92) stitches from the Back stitch holder to the
needle. Join yarn, and purl 1 row.

Shape Armholes

Row 1 K1, ssk, knit to last 3 stitches, k2tog, k1.
Row 2 Purl.

Repeat these 2 rows twice more—60 (64, 74,
82, 86) stitches.

Work in stockinette stitch until piece measures
2 (2, 2½, 3, 3)" (5 [5, 6.5, 7.5, 7.5]cm) from
beginning of armhole shaping, ending with a
wrong-side row.

Purl 1 row on the right side. Work in stockinette
stitch until Back measures the same length as
the Front.

Three-Needle Bind-off

Place the back stitches on 1 needle. Matching the Right Front shoulder stitches to right Back shoulder stitches, place the Right Front stitches on a second needle. Hold the pieces with right sides facing, and using a third needle, knit together 1 stitch each from front and back needles. Repeat, then bind off the first stitch. Continue to bind off all of the right shoulder stitches in this manner.

Slip the next 22 (24, 26, 28, 28) stitches from Back to stitch holder. Repeat the Three-Needle Bind-off for the Left Front and left Back shoulder stitches.

Sleeves

With right side facing and using double-pointed needles or a long circular (page 138 for Magic Loop), join yarn at center of underarm and knit 5 (5, 5, 6, 7) stitches from armhole stitch holder, pick up and knit 66 (65, 70, 76, 75) stitches evenly around armhole, knit 4 (5, 5, 6, 6) remaining stitches from stitch holder—75 (75, 80, 88, 88) stitches.

Place marker, and join for working in the round, being careful not to twist stitches.

Rounds 1–7 Knit.
Round 8 K1, ssk, knit to last 2 stitches before marker, k2tog.

Repeat these 8 rounds 8 more times until 57 (57, 62, 70, 70) stitches remain.

Work even in stockinette stitch until sleeve measures 16½ (16½, 17, 17½, 17½)" (42 [42, 43, 44.5, 44.5]cm) from shoulder seam. Purl 1 round for turning ridge. Work in stockinette stitch for 4 rounds. Bind off.

Mandarin Collar

At turning ridge, fold front facings to the wrong side, and whipstitch them in place. With the right side facing and starting at the Right Front edge, pick up and knit 5 stitches through both the front stitches and the facing, pick up and knit 17 (18, 19, 20, 20) stitches evenly around the right front, knit 22 (24, 26, 28, 28) from Back neck stitch holder, pick up and knit 17 (18, 19, 20, 20) stitches evenly around the Left Front, pick up and knit 5 stitches through the front and facing stitches—66 (70, 74, 78, 78) stitches.

Work 7 rows in stockinette stitch, ending with a wrong-side row. Purl 1 row on the right side for a turning ridge. Work 7 more rows in stockinette stitch. Bind off.

Finishing

Turn jacket and sleeve hems to the wrong side at the turning ridges, and sew in place using a loose whipstitch. Turn the collar to the wrong side at the turning ridge, and whipstitch closed.

Weave in ends. Hand wash in cool water with mild soap (no detergent). Wring and blot to remove excess water, and dry flat.

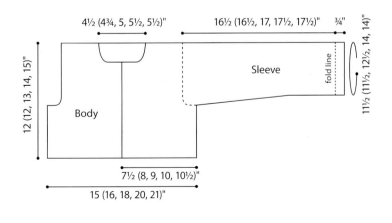

headbands

Skill Level

Easy

Size

One size

Finished Measurements

Width x Length (before felting):
1¼" (3cm) x 19" (48.5cm)
Width x Length (after felting):
1⅛" (2.5cm) x 15" (38cm)

Yarn

▓ 1 skein Harrisville Designs New
England Shetland, 100% pure wool,
1¾ oz (50g), 197 yd (180m), #23
Magenta, **1** super fine

Needles and Notions

▓ US size 5 (3.75mm) circular needle, 40"
(100cm) long, or size needed to obtain
gauge
▓ or US size 5 (3.75mm) set of double-
pointed needles, or size needed to
obtain gauge
▓ Stitch marker
▓ Yarn needle
▓ 1 plastic headband, ½" (13mm) wide
▓ Dressmaker's pencil

Gauge

28 stitches and 35 rounds = 4" (10cm) in
stockinette stitch when worked in the
round, before felting. Adjust needle size
as necessary to obtain correct gauge.

Options, options! Just simple tube knit in the
round, these headbands are super quick
projects. Knit the Felted Headband in an
afternoon, throw it in the washing machine to
felt, then slide it over a plastic headband for a
classic, polished look. Or, for a sporty look,
whip up the Stretchy Headband in no time.
Also knit in the round, it uses leftover yarn from
the Baby Doll Top (page 17) for a quick and
easy little accessory.

Notes

1. The Felted Headband is worked in the round on a
long circular needle (page 138 for Magic Loop), or you
can use double-pointed needles if you prefer.

Felted Headband

Cast on 16 stitches. Place marker, and join for
working in the round, being careful not to twist
stitches. Work in stockinette stitch until piece is 19"
(48.5cm). Bind off.

Finishing

Weave in ends. Felt tube to finished measurements
following instructions in the Felting sidebar (page 49).
Hand wash with warm water and a liquid wool soak.
Wring and blot to remove excess water, and dry flat.

Skill Level

Easy

Size

One size

Finished Measurements

Width: 2" (5cm)
Circumference: 19" (48.5cm)

Yarn

▤ 1 skein Needful Yarns Dubai Stretch, 85% viscose, 15% Elite PBT, 1¾ oz (50g), 182 yd (166m), #109 Lime Green, (❸) light

Needles and Notions

▤ US size 7 (4.5mm) circular needle, 40" (101.5cm) long, or size needed to obtain gauge
▤ or US size 7 (4.5mm) set of double-pointed needles, or size needed to obtain gauge
▤ Yarn needle

Gauge

26 stitches and 40 rounds = 4" (10cm) in stockinette stitch when worked in the round, after washing. Adjust needle size as necessary to obtain correct gauge.

Notes

The Stretchy Headband is worked in the round on a long circular needle (page 138 for Magic Loop), or you can use double-pointed needles if you prefer.

Stretchy Headband

Using a provisional cast-on (page 139) with waste yarn and double-pointed needles or a long circular (page 138 for Magic Loop), cast on 30 stitches. Change to pattern yarn, place marker, and join for working in the round, being careful not to twist stitches.

Work in stockinette stitch for 18" (45.5cm). Carefully remove waste yarn from the cast-on edge, and place stitches on a separate needle.

Three-Needle Bind-off

Line up the second set of stitches to the first set of stitches. Hold the pieces with right sides facing, and using a third needle, knit together 1 stitch each from the front and back needles. Repeat, then bind off the first stitch. Continue to bind off all the stitches in this manner.

Weave in ends. Machine wash on gentle cycle. Wring and blot to remove excess water. Dry flat.

···· it girl style secret

These headbands are so cute and easy that you can make them in as many colors as you like to match just about anything!

ribbed sleeveless top

Skill Level

Easy

Sizes

XS (S, M, L, XL)

Finished Measurements

Bust Circumference (unstretched): 24 (26, 29, 32, 34)" (61 [66, 73.5, 81.5, 86.5]cm)
Length: 18½ (19, 19½, 20, 20½)" (47 [48.5, 49.5, 51, 52]cm)

Yarn

- 5 (5, 6, 7, 7) skeins Southwest Trading Company Vickie Howell Collection Love, 70% bamboo, 30% silk, 1¾ oz (50g), 99 yd (90m), #244 Gale & Dewey, (3) light

Needles and Notions

- US size 6 (4mm) circular needle, 24" (60cm) long, or size needed to obtain gauge
- Stitch holders
- Stitch markers
- Yarn needle

Gauge

26 stitches and 28 rounds = 4" (10cm) in k2, p2 rib (unstretched) when worked in the round. Adjust needle size as necessary to obtain correct gauge.

Notes

1. The Ribbed Sleeveless Top is worked in the round. It is divided into Front and Back at the armholes and worked back and forth in rows.

This top is made with butter-soft silk yarn that knits up quickly on large needles. The easy 2 x 2 ribbing and simple shaping make this top hug your curves, and the circular knitting keeps seaming to a minimum. An easy picked-up collar creates a little sassy attitude. This top is so versatile. You can dress it up or down. Keep it simple with jeans and flats, or wear it to the office or a special event with a pencil skirt and a cute jacket.

2. Use a different colored stitch marker for the beginning of the round.

Abbreviations

M1K: Make 1 stitch by using the bar increase method (page 139), and knitting the increase.
M1P: Make 1 stitch by using the bar increase method (page 139), and purling the increase.

Body

Cast on 156 (168, 188, 208, 220) stitches. Place marker, and join for working in the round, being careful not to twist stitches.

Set-up Round K1, *p2, k2; repeat from * to last 3 stitches, p2, k1.

Waist

Work 78 (84, 94, 104, 110) stitches in pattern, place marker, work to end of round.

Work even until piece measures 2" (5cm) from beginning.

Shape Waist
Round 1 *K1, p2tog, work in pattern to 3 stitches before next marker, p2tog, k1; repeat from * to end once.
Rounds 2–9 Work in pattern.
Repeat these 9 rounds 2 more times—144 (156, 176, 196, 208) stitches.

Round 1 *K1, p1, M1K, p2, work to 4 stitches before next marker, p2, M1K, p1, k1; repeat from * to end once.
Rounds 2–9 Work in pattern.
Round 10 *K1, p1, M1K, k1, p2, work to 5 stitches before next marker, p2, M1K, k1, p1, k1; repeat from * to end once.
Rounds 11–18 Work in pattern.
Round 19 *K1, M1P, p1, k2, p2, work to 6

stitches before next marker, p2, k2, p1, M1P, k1; repeat from * to end once—156 (168, 188, 208, 220) stitches.

Work even in pattern until the piece measures 11" (28cm) from beginning.

Divide for Armholes

Next Row *Work to 6 (6, 7, 9, 9) stitches before next marker, bind off 6 (6, 7, 9, 9) stitches in pattern, remove marker and bind off 6 (6, 7, 9, 9) more stitches; repeat from * to end once.

Left Front

Working back and forth in rows, work on the first 33 (36, 40, 43, 46) stitches only, leaving the remaining stitches unworked for Right Front and Back.

Shape Neck and Armholes

Row 1 (RS) Slip 1 stitch knitwise, k1, ssk (armhole edge), work to last 4 stitches, k2tog, k2 (neck edge).
Rows 2–4 Slip 1 stitch knitwise, work in pattern to end.

Repeat these 4 rows 4 (4, 5, 5, 5) more times— 23 (26, 28, 31, 34) stitches.

Shape Neck

Row 1 (RS) Slip 1 stitch knitwise, work to last 4 stitches, k2tog, k2.
Rows 2–4 Slip 1 stitch knitwise, work in pattern to end.

Repeat these 4 rows 6 (7, 7, 8, 9) more times— 16 (18, 20, 22, 24) stitches.

Work even in pattern until piece measures 18½ (19, 19½, 20, 20½)" (47 [48.5, 49.5, 51, 52]cm) from the cast-on edge. Place stitches on stitch holder to be joined later.

Right Front

With right side facing, join yarn at center of Front, and work on the next 33 (36, 40, 43, 46) stitches only, leaving remaining stitches unworked for Back.

Shape Neck and Armholes

Row 1 (RS) Slip 1 stitch knitwise, k1, ssk (neck edge), work to last 4 stitches, k2tog, k2 (armhole edge).
Rows 2–4 Slip 1 stitch knitwise, work in pattern to end.

Repeat these 4 rows 4 (4, 5, 5, 5) more times— 23 (26, 28, 31, 34) stitches.

Shape Neck

Row 1 (RS) Slip 1 stitch knitwise, k1, ssk, work in pattern to end.

Rows 2–4 Slip 1 stitch knitwise, work in pattern to end.

Repeat these 4 rows 6 (7, 7, 8, 9) more times—16 (18, 20, 22, 24) stitches.

Work even in pattern until piece measures 18½ (19, 19½, 20, 20½)" (47 [48.5, 49.5, 51, 52]cm) from the cast-on edge. Place stitches on stitch holder to be joined later.

Back

With right side facing, join yarn and work the 66 (72, 82, 86, 92) stitches for Back.

Row 1 (RS) Slip 1 stitch knitwise, k1, ssk, work to last 4 stitches, k2tog, k2.

Rows 2–4 Slip 1 stitch knitwise, work in pattern to end.

Repeat these 4 rows 4 more times—56 (62, 68, 74, 80) stitches.

Work even in pattern until piece measures 18½ (19, 19½, 20, 20½)" (47 [48.5, 49.5, 51, 52]cm) from beginning.

Three-Needle Bind-off

Place the Back stitches on 1 needle. Matching the Right Front shoulder stitches to the Right Back shoulder stitches, place the Right Front stitches on a second needle. Hold the pieces with right sides facing, and using a third needle, knit together 1 stitch each from the front and back needles. Repeat, then bind off the first stitch. Continue to bind off all of the right shoulder stitches in this manner.

Slip the next 24 (26, 28, 30, 32) Back stitches to a stitch holder. Repeat the Three-Needle Bind-off for the left shoulder stitches.

Collar

Measure 4½" (11.5cm) down from shoulders along each front neck edge, and mark for beginning and end of the Collar.

With right side facing and starting at Right Front marker, pick up and knit 29 stitches evenly along Right Front, work in pattern across 24 (26, 28, 30, 32) Back stitches from the stitch holder, pick up and knit 29 stitches evenly along the Left Front to the marker—82 (84, 86, 88, 90) stitches total.

Row 1 (RS) Slip 1 stitch knitwise, k2, M1 in pattern (knit or purl), work in pattern to last 3 stitches, M1 in pattern (knit or purl), k3.

Row 2 Slip 1 stitch knitwise, work in pattern to end.

Repeat these 2 rows until collar measures 2½" (6.5cm) from beginning. Bind off in pattern.

Finishing

Weave in ends. Hand wash. Wring and blot to remove excess water, and dry flat.

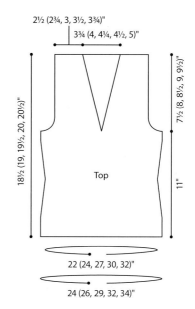

2½ (2¾, 3, 3½, 3¾)"

3¾ (4, 4¼, 4½, 5)"

7½ (8, 8½, 9, 9½)"

18½ (19, 19½, 20, 20½)"

Top

11"

22 (24, 27, 30, 32)"

24 (26, 29, 32, 34)"

lace
cap

Skill Level

Intermediate

Sizes

S (M, L)

Finished Measurements

Head Circumference: 20 (22, 23)" (51 [56, 58.5]cm)

Yarn

▥ 1 skein Southwest Trading Company Vickie Howell Collection Love, 70% bamboo, 30% silk, 1¾ oz (50g), 99 yd (90m), #253 Shelby and Jackson, 🔵 medium

Needles and Notions

▥ US size 8 (5mm) circular needle, 40" (100cm) long, or size needed to obtain gauge
▥ or US size 8 (5mm) pair of double-pointed needles, or size needed to obtain gauge
▥ US size 8 (5mm) circular needle, 16" (40.5cm) long, or size needed to obtain gauge
▥ US size 4 (3.5mm) circular needle, 16" (40.5cm) long
▥ Stitch marker
▥ Yarn needle

Gauge

16 stitches and 26 rounds = 4" (10cm) in pattern stitch when worked in the round. Adjust needle size as necessary to obtain correct gauge.

Here's another one-skein project you can make in an afternoon. A luxurious blend of bamboo and silk really shows off my favorite yarn-over lace stitch that's super easy to learn and quick to knit. And the cap is so cute, you can wear it with any outfit.

Notes

1. The Lace Cap is worked from the top down to the ribbed edge.
2. The spiral at the top of the cap begins with a small number of stitches worked in the round. These can be worked on double-pointed needles or a long circular (page 138 for Magic Loop). When there are enough stitches to go around the shorter circular needle, slip all of the stitches to the short circular needle and work in the round.

Cap

Cast on 8 stitches. Divide stitches in half for the Magic Loop, if using, or distribute stitches evenly over double-pointed needles. Join to begin working in the round, taking care to not twist stitches. Place marker at the beginning of the round.

Round 1 (K1f&b) in each stitch—16 stitches.
Round 2 *Yo, k2tog; repeat from * around.
Round 3 *K1f&b, k1; repeat from * around—24 stitches.
Round 4 *Yo, k2tog; repeat from * around.
Round 5 *K1f&b, k2; repeat from * around—32 stitches.
Round 6 *Yo, k2tog; repeat from * around.
Round 7 *K1f&b, k3; repeat from * around—40 stitches.
Round 8 *Yo, k2tog; repeat from * around.
Round 9 *K1f&b, k4; repeat from * around—48 stitches.
Round 10 *Yo, k2tog; repeat from * around.
Round 11 *K1f&b, k5; repeat from * around—56 stitches.
Round 12 *Yo, k2tog; repeat from * around.
Round 13 K1f&b, k6; repeat from * around—64 stitches.
Round 14 *Yo, k2tog; repeat from * around.

Round 15 *K1f&b, k7; repeat from * around—72 stitches.
Round 16 *Yo, k2tog; repeat from * around.
Round 17 *K1f&b, k8; repeat from * around—80 stitches.

For Size Medium Only
Round 18 *Yo, k2tog; repeat from * around.
Round 19 *K1f&b, k9; repeat from * around—88 stitches

For Size Large Only
Round 18 *Yo, k2tog; repeat from * around.
Round 19 *K1f&b, k10; repeat from * around—92 stitches.

For All Sizes
Repeat **Round 2** for 2½" (6.5cm) more.

Ribbed Band
Change to smaller needle. Work in k2, p2 rib for 2" (5cm). Using larger needles, bind off loosely in rib pattern.

Finishing

Weave in ends. Hand wash. Wring and blot to remove excess water, and dry flat.

it girl style secret

When you're feeling casual, wear the Lace Cap with the Comfy Cotton Pants (page 41) and the Ribbed Sleeveless Top (page 33) for an all-knitted outfit that you can make yourself. This cap also is a perfect dressy accessory with the Sweet and Flirty Empire Dress (page 61).

comfy cotton pants

Skill Level

Intermediate

Sizes

XS (S, M, L, XL)

Finished Measurements

Hip Circumference: 30 (32, 36, 40, 42)" (76 [81, 91, 101.5, 106.5]cm)
Inseam Length: 31 (32, 32, 33, 34)" (79 [81, 81, 84, 86]cm)

Yarn

▓ 13 (15, 17, 20, 22) balls of Crystal Palace Yarns Bamboozle, 55% bamboo, 24% cotton, 21% elastic nylon, 1¾ oz (50g), 90 yd (82m), #0204 Ivory, ④ medium

Needles and Notions

▓ US size 7 (4.5mm) circular needle, 24" (61cm) long
▓ US size 8 (5mm) circular needle, 24" (61cm) long, or size needed to obtain gauge
▓ US size 8 (5mm) circular needle, 16" (40cm) long, or size needed to obtain gauge
▓ Stitch markers
▓ Stitch holders
▓ Yarn needle
▓ 4 yd (3.6m) elastic thread (3mm)
▓ Sewing needle and thread

Gauge

19 stitches and 28 rounds = 4" (10cm) in stockinette stitch on US size 8 (5mm) when worked in the round.
Adjust needle size as necessary to obtain correct gauge.

You won't believe how comfortable these knitted pants are. The amazing bamboo-cotton blend yarn is extremely stretchy, soft, and light. Worked completely in the round, these pants are easy-to-knit straight tubes. The legs have no shaping to slow you down, and the low-riding 2 x 2 ribbed waistband can be adjusted to fit perfectly. If you've ever wanted a pair of pants that fit like a glove, with classy drape and killer style, then make them yourself with this easy pattern. Even a beginner can master these.

Notes

1. The Legs are worked separately in the round and then joined.
2. Short rows (page 139) are used to add some fullness to the back of the pants. Each short row is actually 2 partial rows (Wrap and Turn, page 139) sandwiched between 3 full rounds (described in Steps 1 and 2). Each time you work Steps 1 and 2, you add about ¼" (6mm) in height to the back. By repeating Steps 1 and 2, you can add as many inches as you like.
3. To adjust the pant length, slip leg stitches onto a waste yarn and try on the pants to determine how many more inches to work. Return the stitches to the needle, and work as many rows as desired until the beginning of the shaping where the legs are joined.

Leg (Make 2)

With the shorter US size 8 (5mm) circular needle, cast on 78 (82, 94, 104, 110) stitches loosely. Place marker, and join for working in the round, being careful not to twist the stitches.

Work in stockinette stitch until the piece measures 31 (32, 32, 33, 34)" (78.5 [81, 81, 84, 86.5]cm) or the desired length from the cast-on edge (see customization instructions in Notes above).

On the last round, knit to 2 (3, 3, 3, 4) stitches before the marker, work (M1, k1) 5 (7, 7, 8, 9) times to increase for leg join—83 (89, 101, 112, 119) stitches.

Slip all stitches to a stitch holder.

Join Legs

Slip the next 12 (13, 15, 17, 19) stitches from the second Leg onto a stitch holder, and slip all but 12 (14, 16, 18, 20) stitches from the first Leg onto the needles. The stitches on holders will be joined later as the leg join using a Three-Needle Bind-off.

Hold the Leg pieces together at the inseam stitches, with right sides facing. With the longer US size 8 (5mm) circular needle, knit all remaining stitches from both Legs, and join for working in the round—142 (152, 172, 190, 200) stitches total.

Work in stockinette stitch for 2 (3, 4, 5, 6)" (5 [7.5, 10, 12.5, 15]cm).

Divide stitches in half, and place stitch markers at sides of hips so that 71 (76, 86, 95, 100) stitches are in the front and 71 (76, 86, 95, 100) stitches are in the back. Use different colored stitch markers to designate the first marker as Marker 1 and the second as Marker 2.

Short Row Shaping

Short rows are worked across the back stitches in stockinette stitch between Markers 1 and 2. The front stitches wait on the needle while short rows are worked, and then all hip stitches are worked in the round for 3 rounds between each set of short rows.

Step 1: Knit to 1 stitch before Marker 2. Wrap next stitch, turn work around and purl back to 1 stitch before Marker 1. Wrap and turn.

Step 2: Return to working in the round across back stitches (the stitches between Markers 1 and 2), and continue around entire hip circumference, picking up the wraps and working them together with the next stitches as you pass them. Work 2 more rounds in stockinette stitch, ending at Marker 1.

Repeat Steps 1 and 2, each time working to 3 stitches before the previous wrapped stitch, until 4 stitches have been wrapped on each side.

Work even in stockinette stitch until the back measures 6 (7, 8, 9, 10)" (15 [18, 20.5, 23, 25.5]cm) from the leg join.

On the last round, decrease 2 (0, 0, 2, 0) stitches evenly using k2tog—140 (152, 172, 188, 200) stitches total.

Change to US size 7 (4.5mm) circular needle and work in k2, p2 rib for 2" (5cm). Bind off loosely in rib.

Finishing

With a yarn needle, thread 4 rows of elastic thread along wrong side of ribbed waistband, being careful not to let the elastic show on the right side. Pull elastic snug to fit, and secure in place with a knot.

Three-Needle Bind-off

With wrong side facing, pick up and knit 1 stitch from the body of the garment, slip 12 (13, 15, 17, 19) stitches from 1 leg join stitch holder onto needle, pick up and knit 1 stitch from body of garment—14 (15, 17, 19, 21) stitches.

Repeat for the second set of crotch stitches, picking up and knitting 1 stitch from pants at the beginning, slipping stitches onto a second needle, and knitting 1 stitch from pants at the end. Hold the pieces with right sides facing, and using a third needle, knit together 1 stitch each from front and back needles. Repeat, then bind off the first stitch. Continue to bind off all the leg join stitches in this manner.

Weave in ends. Hand wash or machine wash with cool water in the gentle cycle. Wring and blot to remove excess water, and dry flat.

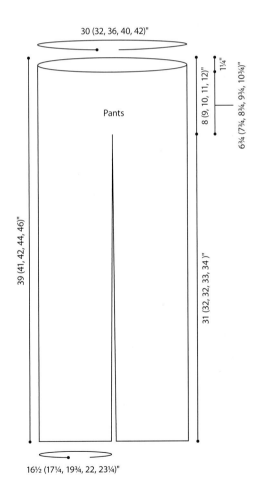

30 (32, 36, 40, 42)"

Pants

1¼"

8 (9, 10, 11, 12)"

6¾ (7¾, 8¾, 9¾, 10¾)"

39 (41, 42, 44, 46)"

31 (32, 32, 33, 34)"

16½ (17¼, 19¾, 22, 23¼)"

felted
it bag

Skill Level

Easy

Size

One size

Finished Measurements

Height x Width x Depth (before felting):
12" (30.5cm) x 13½" (34.5cm) x 6¼"
(16cm) deep
Height x Width x Depth (after felting): 8½"
(21.5cm) x 11" (28cm) x 5" (12.5cm) deep

Yarn

▦ 5 skeins Nashua Handknits Creative
Focus Chunky, 75% wool, 25% alpaca,
3½ oz (100g), 110 yd (100m), #3743
Turquoise, ⑤ bulky

Needles and Notions

▦ US size 10 (6mm) knitting needles, or
size needed to obtain gauge
▦ Yarn needle
▦ 1 yd (1m) brocade fabric (for strap and
optional lining)
▦ Sewing needle and thread to match
fabric color
▦ Dressmaker's pencil
▦ Straight pins
▦ Grommet hole cutter tool (optional) or
scissors
▦ 2 large round top, spring door purse
rings, nickel color
▦ 4 heavy grommets, silver color
▦ Grommet setting tool
▦ 1 sew-on snap, size 7, nickel color

Worked in quick-to-knit garter stitch panels, this project is simple and super stylish! With a simple brocade fabric handle and optional fashion details, this bag incorporates crafty skills like sewing, beading, and jewelry making. The Felted It Bag's optional details include hot style features like chains and charms, with instructions for making a custom jeweled purse chain featuring sterling silver alphabet charms to spell anything you want.

Jeweled Chain Notions (Optional)

▦ Clear Accu-Flex® Beading Wire,
49-strand, 0.024 (.6mm)diameter
▦ 2 jump rings, 10.9mm, 17 gauge, stainless steel
▦ 2 crimps, cut tube, 3 x 2mm, sterling silver
▦ 1 each of alphabet heart bead, 5.5mm, sterling
silver, letters I, T, G, I, R, and L
▦ 3 Swarovski® Crystal Beads Faceted Rondelle,
6mm, Crystal AB
▦ 7 Swarovski® Crystal Beads Faceted Rondelle,
6mm, Caribbean Blue Opal
▦ 5 Swarovski® Crystal Beads Faceted Round,
10mm, Crystal AB
▦ 8 Swarovski® Crystal Beads Faceted Round, 8mm,
Crystal AB
▦ 3 Swarovski® Crystal Beads Faceted Round, 6mm,
Crystal AB
▦ 1 Swarovski® Crystal Bead Faceted Round, 8mm,
Fuchsia
▦ 7 Swarovski® Crystal Beads Faceted Round, 6mm,
Tanzanite

- 4 Swarovski® Crystal Beads Faceted Bicone, 6mm, Rose
- 3 Swarovski® Crystal Beads Faceted Bicone, 6mm, Amethyst
- 4 Swarovski® Crystal Beads Faceted Bicone, 6mm, Capri Blue
- 3 Swarovski® Crystal Beads Faceted Bicone, 6mm, Light Rose
- 1 Swarovski® Crystal Bead Faceted Bicone, 6mm, Light Amethyst
- 2 Swarovski® Crystal Bead Faceted Bicone, 6mm, Fuchsia
- Chain-nose pliers

Chain Notions (Optional)

- 4 Jump rings, 10.9mm, 17 gauge, stainless steel
- Twisted cable chain, 11 x 6mm, silver finish
- Chain-nose pliers
- Metal-cutting pliers

Dangling Jeweled Chain Notions (Optional)

- 2" (5cm) length of curb chain, 4mm, silver finish
- 1 Jump ring, 10.9mm, 17 gauge, stainless steel
- 3 Swarovski® Crystal Beads Faceted Heart, 10.3 x 10mm, rose
- 1 Swarovski® Crystal Bead Faceted Heart, 14.4 x 14mm, blue zircon
- 1 each Clematis, Heart with Cut-out, and Shoe charm, pewter
- 7 Jump rings, 6.5mm round, stainless steel
- 1 Pendant bail, silver plated
- Chain-nose pliers
- Metal-cutting pliers

Heart Charm Notions (Optional)

- Twisted cable chain, 6 x 11mm, silver finish
- 2 jump rings, 10.9mm, 17 gauge, stainless steel
- 1 heart charm (locket or plain), large, sterling silver
- 1 pendant bail, ice pick style, silver plated
- Chain-nose pliers
- Metal-cutting pliers

Gauge

14 stitches and 32 rows = 4" (10cm) in garter stitch when worked flat, before felting.
Adjust needle size as necessary to obtain correct gauge.

Sides (Make 2)

Cast on 47 stitches. Work in garter stitch for 12" (30.5cm). Bind off.

Ends (Make 2)

Cast on 22 stitches. Work in garter stitch for 12" (30.5cm). Bind off.

Bottom

Cast on 47 stitches. Work in garter stitch for 6¼" (16cm). Bind off.

Finishing

Using yarn and yarn needle, whipstitch pieces together. Weave in ends.

Following instructions on felting (page 49), felt the bag to the finished measurements. Check it often to control the amount of the felting. When it reaches the correct size, remove it from the washer to the sink or tub and rinse it in cold water. Squeeze out excess water. Pull the bag into shape while it is still wet.

Block the bag into shape while it's drying. Fill the bag with as many items needed to stretch the bottom and sides to the specified dimensions, and set the bag aside to air-dry.

Make Strap

Cut a piece of brocade 36" (91.5cm) long and 7" (18cm) wide. With cool iron and a pressing cloth over the fabric, press the fabric smooth. Lay the fabric on the table and fold in half lengthwise with right sides together. Either by hand or with a sewing machine, sew the long side and both ends, using a ½" (13mm) seam allowance all around and leaving a 3" (7.5cm) opening in the center of the length for turning the strap to the right side. Turn the strap to the right side, and carefully sew the opening closed. Fold over ends 1" (2.5cm) to make a casing for purse rings to slide through, and sew.

Attach Hardware

To determine correct grommet placement on the side panels of the purse, measure ¾" (2cm) down from the top edge and mark spots 3" (7.5cm) apart from each other, centered on the side panel, with a dressmaker's pencil. Then place 2 straight pins in the shape of a cross with the center of the cross being the hole for the grommet. Once you have pinned the placement of both sets of grommets and have checked the placement for evenness and symmetry (this can be a bit tricky, because felting will sometimes make the bag a bit uneven or lopsided), cut a ½" (13mm) cross with scissors at the center of each pair of pins (or use a grommet hole cutting tool, if you have one). Carefully cut away the felted wool to the inside circumference of the grommets. Coat the inside edge of your wool holes with glue to secure the fabric. Using the grommet setting tool, attach the grommets. Set aside to dry overnight.

Assembly

Slide the purse rings into the casings at each end of the fabric strap. Pinching the large sides of the purse together to make a vertical fold in the side panel, line up the grommets, and slide the purse rings through the grommets. Sew the large snap to the center of the inside edge of purse, ½" (13mm) from the top edge.

Lining (Optional)

From the brocade, cut 2 pieces to the same dimensions as the felted bag sides, adding ½" (13mm) around each piece for a seam allowance and rounding the corners along the bottom edge. Either by hand or with a sewing machine, sew pieces together using a ½" (13mm) seam allowance. Either sew in the purse lining before sewing on hardware, or insert the lining last, as I did.

If you put the lining in first, place it in the purse and fold down the top edge of the lining to the height you want it—a ½" (13mm) margin from the top edge of the purse looks very tidy. If you put your lining in last, fold down the lining to 9½" (24cm) high from the bottom of the lining. After folding down for either version, press fold line with a cool iron and topstitch ⅛" (3mm) from top edge to hold in place.

To sew in the liner, turn the purse inside out, and slip in the lining so that the right side is facing out. Pin liner in place, measuring from the top edge of purse to make sure that the lining is evenly attached. Sew lining to purse by stitching along the top edge very close to the seam at the top of the lining. Turn purse to the right side, and push lining down inside. Tack lightly along bottom to hold lining down.

Jeweled Chain (Optional)

Cut a 14" (35.5cm) length of beading wire, and slide a crimp tube and a jump ring onto 1 end. Tuck the wire down into the crimp tube, and slide the jump ring and crimp tube to the end of the wire, leaving a ⅛" (3mm) loop in the beading wire between the crimp tube and the jump ring. With chain-nose pliers, squeeze the crimp tube to flatten.

String beads onto the wire in this order: Caribbean Blue Opal rondelle, Crystal AB round 6mm, Rose Bicone, Crystal AB round 8mm, Capri Blue bicone, Tanzanite 6mm, Crystal AB round 10mm, Fuchsia bicone, Crystal AB round 6mm, Caribbean Blue Opal rondelle, Tanzanite 6mm, Crystal AB 6mm rondelle, Rose bicone, Fuchsia bicone, Crystal AB 8mm, Light Amethyst bicone, Capri Blue bicone, Crystal AB 8mm, Caribbean Blue Opal rondelle, Amethyst bicone, Crystal AB 10mm, Light Rose bicone, Crystal AB 6mm, L alphabet bead, Tanzanite 6mm, R alphabet bead, Tanzanite 6mm, I alphabet bead, Tanzanite 6mm, G alphabet bead, Tanzanite 6mm, T alphabet bead, Tanzanite 6mm, I alphabet bead, Crystal AB 8mm, Capri Blue bicone, Crystal AB 10mm, Caribbean Blue Opal rondelle, Fuchsia round 8mm, Crystal AB

10mm, Caribbean Blue Opal rondelle, Crystal AB 10mm, Caribbean Blue Opal rondelle, Crystal AB 8mm, Capri Blue bicone, Amethyst bicone, Light Rose bicone, Crystal AB rondelle, Rose bicone, Caribbean Blue Opal rondelle, Crystal AB 8mm, Rose bicone, Crystal AB rondelle, Light Rose bicone, Amethyst bicone, Crystal AB 8mm, Crystal AB 8mm.

Slide on a crimp tube and a jump ring. Repeat the procedure for crimping tube to fasten end of jeweled chain.

Chains (Optional)

Cut 1 piece of twisted cable chain 14" (35.5cm) long. Cut a second piece 15½" (39.5cm) long. Attach jump rings to each end of both chains.

Dangling Jeweled Chain (Optional)

Cut a 2" (5cm) length of twisted cable chain and attach the largest jump ring to 1 end. Attach jump rings to all charms except the large blue heart. Attach pendant bail to large

heart and a jump ring to the pendant bail. Lay chain on table, and place all charms beside chain to determine where to attach them. With jump ring at 1 end (this will be the top of the chain), arrange the charms in this order: pink heart, pewter charm, pink heart, pewter charm, pink heart, pewter charm, and the large blue heart, which will dangle at the end of the chain. Attach charms to chain with their jump rings.

Heart Charm (Optional)

Cut a 1" (2.5cm) length of twisted cable chain, and attach jump rings to each end. Attach the ice pick pendant bail to the heart charm and attach to 1 jump ring.

Assembly

Holding the left jump ring firmly in your hand, open the hinge and slide the 2 chains on, longest first, then the Jeweled Chain, the Heart Charm, and the Dangling Jeweled Chain. Close ring. Repeat on right side for the remaining chain

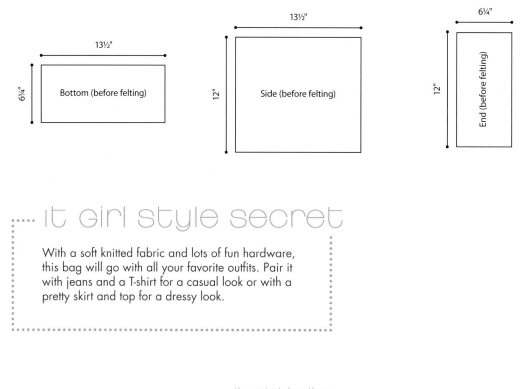

13½"

Bottom (before felting)

6¼"

13½"

Side (before felting)

12"

6¼"

End (before felting)

12"

1. Pick Your Yarn

   Your yarn must contain mostly animal fibers. Look for blends that are at least 70%—preferably at least 80%—animal fibers like alpaca, angora, camel, qiviut, and wool. Stay away from "superwash" wool, which has been treated to prevent felting.

2. Felt

   Felting is the process of making the yarn fibers grab onto each other and interlock to become a completely different fabric. You make this happen with three key ingredients: hot water, agitation, and laundry detergent. You can felt your yarn in a washing machine (top or front loader) or by hand. Washing machines make felting a relatively painless process, but hand felting allows the most control. Let's take a look at the different methods and how to use each.

   Top-Loading Washing Machine

   Put your project in the washing machine (in a zippered lingerie bag if the project is small or one that's long and skinny and likely to get twisted around something and pulled out of shape) with some heavy items like jeans (make sure they are old and won't bleed) and a bit of detergent. Turn the wash cycle to the longest hottest setting. Set a timer for about 10 minutes, and turn on the washer. After 10 minutes, stop the washer and pull out your project to check for the degree of felting. Look for a loss of stitch definition and a matting of the fibers. Measure it with a measuring tape. If it has not yet reached the finished measurements for the project, throw it back in and let it whirl some more, checking every 5 minutes or so for felting progress. The project can go from huge to microscopic in a flash, so check it frequently. To avoid permanent creasing in the knitted fabric, do not let the spin cycle start while the project is in the washer.

   Felting by Hand

   Drop your project in a sink, bucket, tub, or any other container with hot water, and get the yarn good and wet. Take the project out of the water, lay it on top of something rough (e.g., a bamboo mat, washboard, or towel), and add a small amount of laundry detergent and just enough HOT water to keep things squishy. Now put on some rubber gloves and rub! Rub the yarn against itself and against the rough surface. Be sure to keep the felting project hot (by adding a bit of hot water as you work), but don't rinse away the soap. Keep your measuring tape nearby, and check the progress once you see the characteristic matting and hardening of fibers.

3. Rinse

   Rinse the project in cold water until the water runs clear. Squeeze out as much water as you can, taking care to not crease the felted fabric. Lay the felt between 2 clean towels and press hard on the top towel to blot the water. Repeat with more clean dry towels until little water remains.

4. Block

   Place your wet project on a piece of foam board (mat board or cardboard will work, too), pull all the edges to the finished dimensions listed on the pattern, and pin the edges down so that the pins hold the shape while the project dries. The felt will hold its shape after it's dry, so make sure that you pull and push the edges and sides to get just the shape or dimensions desired. With 3-dimensional objects (like purses), you'll need to use an assortment of objects to make the right shape. I grab cereal boxes, plastic boxes, or even cut pieces of mat board or foam board to make the sides straight and the bottom corners crisp. Cover all nonplastic forms with plastic grocery bags. Once you've got the shape-making forms or pins in place, leave the project to dry.

   For more felting tips, visit phoenixbess.com.

days off

Days off are about sleeping in, playing at the beach, and eating too much ice cream. The designs in this section are perfect for being lazy and having fun, which is what I do best when I don't have a book to write or math homework to finish. These garments make me feel good. They're comfortable without being slouchy. On your days off, you can knit a variety of fun fashions to wear wherever your social calendar takes you.

boyfriend sweater

Skill Level

Easy

Sizes

XS (S, M, L, XL)

Finished Measurements

Bust Circumference: 42 (44, 48, 51½, 54)"
(106.5 [112, 122, 131, 137]cm)
Body Length (from shoulder to hem): 21
(21½, 22, 22½, 23)" (53.5 [54.5, 56, 57,
58.5]cm)

Yarn

- 13 (14, 15, 17, 18) skeins Bernat
  Bamboo, 86% bamboo, 12% acrylic,
  2% polyester, 2.1oz (60g), 63 yd (57m),
  #92425 Rosehip, (5) bulky

Needles and Notions

- US size 10.5 (6.5mm) circular needle,
  24" (61cm) long, or size needed to
  obtain gauge
- US size 10.5 (6.5mm) circular needle,
  40" (101.5cm) long, or size needed to
  obtain gauge
- or US size 10.5 (6.5mm) double-
  pointed needles, or size needed to
  obtain gauge
- Stitch holders
- Stitch markers
- Yarn needle

Gauge

13 stitches and 20 rounds = 4" (10cm) in
stockinette stitch when worked in the
round. Adjust needle size as necessary to
obtain correct gauge.

This sweater is so big, loose, and comfortable
that you'll reach for it every day. Made in an
incredibly soft and chunky bamboo yarn, it
knits up quickly on big needles and features an
easy seamless construction that makes it a
perfect first-sweater project. The collar is sharp
and crisp looking, and knitting it is a breeze
with simple double decreases that any novice
knitter can handle.

Notes

1. The Boyfriend Sweater is worked from the bottom
up, in the round on circular needles, to the armholes. It
is then divided for the front and back sections and
worked back and forth in rows. Each Sleeve is picked
up from the armhole edge and worked down to the
cuff on double-pointed needles or a long circular
(page 138 for Magic Loop).
2. The double decrease in the Neckband should be
worked as follows: Slip 2 stitches together knitwise, k1,
pass the 2 slipped stitches over.

Body

With the shorter circular needle, cast on 136 (144,
156, 168, 176) stitches. Place marker, and join for
working in the round, being careful not to twist
stitches. Work in k2, p2 rib for 5 rounds. Change to
stockinette stitch and work until piece measures 14"
(35.5cm) from beginning.

Divide for Armholes

*Knit 2 (2, 2, 4, 4) stitches and place them on a stitch
holder, knit 66 (70, 76, 80, 84) stitches and slip
stitches to a stitch holder for Back; repeat from * to
end once more, leaving the 66 (70, 76, 80, 84)
stitches on the needle for the Front.

You will have 2 (2, 2, 4, 4) stitches on holders at each side for armholes and 66 (70, 76, 80, 84) stitches each for the Front and Back.

Front

Working back and forth on the 66 (70, 76, 80, 84) Front stitches only, work even in stockinette stitch for 1½ (2, 2½, 3, 3½)" (4 [5, 6.5, 7.5, 9]cm), ending with a wrong-side row. Divide the stitches in half, placing a marker between center 2 stitches.

Shape Neck for Left Front
Work on the first 33 (35, 38, 40, 42) stitches only.

Row 1 Knit to 3 stitches before marker, k2tog, k1.
Row 2 Purl.

Repeat these 2 rows 12 times more—20 (22, 25, 27, 29) stitches.

Work even in stockinette stitch until piece measures 7 (7½, 8, 8½, 9)" (18 [19, 20.5, 21.5, 23]cm) from armhole. Place stitches on a stitch holder for the shoulder.

Shape Neck for Right Front
With right side facing, join yarn to work the remaining 33 (35, 38, 40, 42) stitches.

Row 1 K1, ssk, knit to end.
Row 2 Purl.

Repeat these 2 rows 12 times more—20 (22, 25, 27, 29) stitches.

Work even in stockinette stitch until the piece measures 7 (7½, 8, 8½, 9)" (18 [19, 20.5, 21.5, 23]cm) from the armhole. Place stitches on stitch holder for the shoulder.

Back

Slip the 66 (70, 76, 80, 84) stitches from the stitch holder for the Back to the needle. With right side facing, join yarn and work back and forth in stockinette stitch until piece measures 7 (7½, 8, 8½, 9)" (18 [19, 20.5, 21.5, 23]cm) from armhole.

Three-Needle Bind-off
Place the Back stitches on 1 needle. Matching the Right Front shoulder stitches to right Back shoulder stitches, place the Right Front stitches on a second needle. Hold the pieces with right sides facing, and using a third needle, knit together 1 stitch each from Front and Back needles. Repeat, then bind off the first stitch. Continue to bind off all the right shoulder stitches in this manner.

Slip the next 26 stitches for the Back to a stitch holder. Repeat the Three-Needle Bind-off with the Left Front and Left Back stitches.

Sleeves

With double-pointed needles or a long circular (page 138 for Magic Loop), starting at the center of the underarm, knit 1 (1, 1, 2, 2) stitch(es) from the underarm stitch holder, pick up and knit 46 (48, 52, 56, 58) stitches evenly around the armhole, knit 1 (1, 1, 2, 2) stitch(es) from holder—48 (50, 54, 60, 62) stitches.

Place marker, and join for working in the round, being careful not to twist stitches.

Rounds 1–9 Knit.
Round 10 K1, ssk, knit to last 2 stitches before marker, k2tog.

Repeat these 10 rounds 7 (8, 8, 9, 8) more times until 32 (32, 36, 40, 44) stitches remain.

Work even in stockinette stitch until the Sleeve measures 19 (19, 20, 21, 21)" (48.5 [48.5, 51, 53.5, 53.5]cm) from the shoulder seam. Work in k2, p2 rib for 5 rounds. Bind off in rib.

Neckband

With right side facing, join yarn at the right shoulder, and knit 26 stitches from the Back holder. Pick up and knit 26 stitches along left side of neckline, make 1 stitch between center 2 stitches, pick up and knit 26 stitches along right side of neckline—79 stitches.

Round 1 (P2, k2) 12 times, p2, k1, work double decrease (see Notes on page 53), k1, (p2, k2) 6 times.

Work 5 more rounds, continuing in rib pattern and working the double decrease at the center of the Neckband every round. Bind off in rib, working a double decrease at the center of the Neckband as stitches are bound off.

Finishing

Weave in ends. Hand wash. Wring and blot to remove excess water, and dry flat.

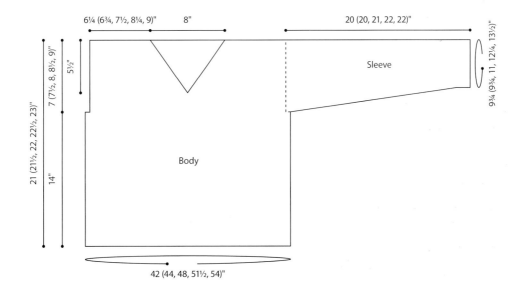

capri pants

Skill Level

Easy

Sizes

XS (S, M, L, XL)

Finished Measurements

Hip Circumference: 30¼ (32½, 36½, 40½, 42¾)" (77 [82.5, 92.5, 103, 108.5]cm)
Inseam Length: 20½ (21, 21½, 22, 22½)" (52 [53.5, 54.5, 56, 57]cm)

Yarn

■ 8 (9, 10, 11, 12) skeins Plymouth Yarn Co. Jeannee, 51% cotton, 49% acrylic, 1¾ oz (50g), 110 yd (100m), #14 White, (**4**) medium

Needles and Notions

■ US size 7 (4.5mm) circular needle, 16" (40.5cm) long, or size needed to obtain gauge
■ US size 7 (4.5mm) circular needle, 24" (61cm) long, or size needed to obtain gauge
■ Stitch holders
■ Stitch markers
■ Yarn needle
■ 1 yd (1m) waistband elastic, ½" (13mm) wide
■ Sewing needle and thread

Gauge

18 stitches and 24 rounds = 4" (10cm) in stockinette stitch when worked in the round.
Adjust needle size as necessary to obtain correct gauge.

These casual pants feature an easy-care cotton blend that is light, soft, and stretchy—and machine washable. Very simple circular construction makes them a great project for beginners, and with details like a customizable elastic waistband and 2 x 2 ribbed cuffs, they will feel and wear like a dream.

Notes

1. Legs are worked separately in the round and then joined.
2. Short rows (page 139) are used to add some fullness to the back of the pants. Each short row is actually 2 partial rows (Wrap and Turn, page 139) sandwiched between 3 full rounds (described in Steps 1 and 2). Each time you work Steps 1 and 2, you add about ¼" (6mm) in height to the back. By repeating Steps 1 and 2, you can add as many inches as you like.
3. To make the pants just the right length, determine how many inches you need to work. Simply slip the Leg stitches onto waste yarn and try on the pants. Return the stitches to the needle, and add as many rows as desired until the beginning of the shaping where the legs are joined.

Leg (Make 2)

With shorter circular needles, cast on 88 (96, 108, 120, 128) stitches. Place marker, and join for working in the round, being careful not to twist the stitches. Work in k2, p2 rib for 1" (2.5cm).

Change to stockinette stitch, decreasing 8 (9, 10, 11, 12) stitches evenly around on the first round—80 (87, 98, 109, 116) stitches.

Work even in stockinette stitch until the piece measures 20½ (21, 21½, 22, 22½)" (52 [53.5, 54.5, 56, 57]cm) or the desired length from the cast-on edge.

Slip all stitches to a stitch holder.

Join Legs

Slip the next 12 (14, 16, 18, 20) stitches from the second Leg onto a stitch holder, and slip all but 12 (14, 16, 18, 20) stitches from the first Leg onto the needles. The stitches on holders will be joined later as the crotch using Three-Needle Bind-off.

Hold the Leg pieces together at the stitches where the legs join, with right sides facing. With the longer circular needle, knit join the stitches from both legs for working in the round—136 (146, 164, 182, 192) stitches.

Work in stockinette stitch for 3 (4, 5, 6, 7)" (7.5 [10, 12.5, 15, 18]cm).

Divide the stitches in half front to back, and place stitch markers at sides of hips so that 68 (73, 82, 91, 96) stitches are in the front and 68 (73, 82, 91, 96) stitches are in the back. Use different colored stitch markers to designate the first marker as Marker 1 and the second as Marker 2.

Short Row Shaping

Short rows are worked across the back stitches in stockinette stitch between Markers 1 and 2. The front stitches wait on the needle while short rows are worked, and all hip stitches are worked in the round for 3 rounds between each set of short rows.

Step 1: Knit to 1 stitch before Marker 2. Wrap and turn (page 139), and purl back to 1 stitch before Marker 1. Wrap and turn.

Step 2: Work in the round across the back stitches (between Markers 1 and 2), continuing around the entire hip circumference, picking up the wraps and working them together with the stitches they wrap as you pass them. Work 2 more rounds in stockinette stitch on all the stitches, ending at Marker 1.

Repeat Steps 1 and 2, each time working to 2 stitches before previous wrapped stitch until 4 stitches have been wrapped at each side.

Work even in stockinette stitch until back measures 7¾ (8¾, 9¾, 10¾, 11¾)" (19.5 [22, 25, 27.5, 30]cm) from crotch. Purl 1 round on the right side to make a turning ridge. Work in stockinette stitch for 1" (2.5cm). Bind off.

it girl style secret

I love how comfortable the Capri Pants are with a bandeau top or the Boyfriend Sweater (page 53). They look especially cute with flip-flops or sandals.

Finishing

Fold the waistband to the wrong side of the garment at the turning ridge. Using a yarn needle and matching yarn, whipstitch the bound-off edge to the wrong side, leaving an opening large enough to slide in the waistband elastic; do not break yarn. Cut the elastic 1" (2.5cm) longer than your waist measurement. Feed the elastic through the casing, pulling out both ends. Overlap the elastic ends by 1" (2.5cm), and sew them together with a sewing needle and thread. Slide the elastic back into the casing, and sew the casing closed with the yarn needle and yarn.

Three-Needle Bind-off

With wrong side facing, pick up and knit 1 stitch from the body of the garment, slip 12 (14, 16, 18, 20) stitches from 1 crotch stitch holder onto needle, pick up and knit 1 stitch from body of garment—14 (16, 18, 20, 22) stitches.

Repeat for the second set of crotch stitches, picking up and knitting 1 stitch from pants at the beginning, slipping stitches onto a second needle, and knitting 1 stitch from pants at the end. Hold the pieces with right sides facing, and using a third needle, knit together 1 stitch each from the first and second needles. Repeat, then bind off the first stitch. Continue to bind off all the leg join stitches in this manner.

Weave in ends. Machine wash on the gentle cycle, and tumble dry on low heat setting.

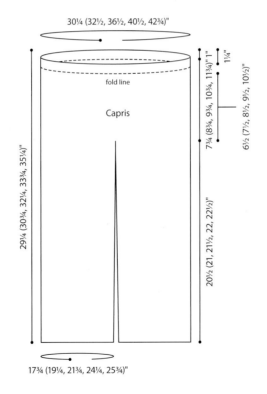

30¼ (32½, 36½, 40½, 42¾)"

fold line

Capris

7¾ (8¾, 9¾, 10¾, 11¾)" 1"

1¼"

6½ (7½, 8½, 9½, 10½)"

29¼ (30¾, 32¼, 33¾, 35¼)"

20½ (21, 21½, 22, 22½)"

17¾ (19¼, 21¾, 24¼, 25¾)"

sweet and flirty empire dress

Skill Level

Intermediate

Sizes

XS (S, M, L, XL)

Finished Measurements

Empire Waist Circumference (just under the bust): 22 (24½, 26½, 29, 31)" (56 [62, 67, 74, 79]cm)

Length (from underarm): 27¼ (27¼, 27¼, 27¾, 27¾)" (69 [69, 69, 70.5, 70.5]cm)

Yarn

- 10 (11, 12, 13, 14) skeins Berroco Ultra Silk, 20% silk, 40% rayon, 40% nylon, 1¾ oz (50g), 98 yd (90m), #6140 Pink Lady, (4) medium

Needles and Notions

- US size 10 (6mm) circular needle, 24" (61cm) long, or size needed to obtain gauge
- US size 10 (6mm) needles, or size needed to obtain gauge (optional)
- Stitch markers
- Yarn needle
- US size F-5 (3.75mm) crochet hook
- ½ yd (47.5cm) elastic, ½" (13mm) wide

I designed this dress to be the highlight of your casual knitted wardrobe. Fitted in all the right places, it hugs your curves and hangs just right. Short and cute, with an easy knitted lace hem, it features a surplice bodice for perfectly classic lines. The yarn is a silk blend that has wonderful drape and works up quickly and seamlessly in the round on larger needles, so you'll enjoy knitting this dress as much as you'll enjoy wearing it.

Lining Notions (Optional)

- 1 pair Sew Sassy Clarissa Bra Cups in appropriate size
- ½ yd (0.5m) lining fabric
- Sewing needle and thread

Gauge

18 stitches and 30 rounds = 4" (10cm) in stockinette stitch when worked in the round. Adjust needle size as necessary to obtain correct gauge.

Notes

1. The Left Cup and the Right Cup are worked back and forth in rows in separate pieces. Optional straight needles may be used for the pieces knitted flat in rows.

2. The Back Inset piece is worked separately, back and forth in rows. Stitches are added for the front, and the

Dress Body is worked in the round from the bust to the hem.

3. The Dress Body is divided into 10 sections with stitch markers. Use a different colored stitch marker for the beginning of the round.

4. All increases are made using the raised increase technique and knitting into the back loop of the raised stitch.

Scalloped Edging Pattern (worked over a multiple of 9 stitches)

Round 1 *Ssk, k5, k2tog, yo; repeat from * to end.
Round 2 *K7, (k1, p1) in yo; repeat from * to end.
Round 3 *Ssk, k3, k2tog, (yo, k1) twice, yo; repeat from * to end.
Round 4 Knit.
Round 5 *Ssk, k1, k2tog, (yo, k1) 5 times, yo; repeat from * to end.
Round 6 *K3, p11; repeat from * to end.
Round 7 *Slip 1, k2tog, psso, yo, k11, yo; repeat from * to end.
Round 8 Bind off purlwise.

Left Cup

Cast on 45 (50, 55, 60, 65) stitches.

Row 1 (RS) Knit to last 3 stitches, k2tog, k1.

Rows 2–4 Work in stockinette stitch.

Repeat these 4 rows 5 (5, 5, 6, 6) more times—39 (44, 49, 53, 58) stitches.

Shape Armhole
Bind off 8 (8, 9, 10, 11) stitches at the beginning of the next right-side row for underarm—31 (36, 40, 43, 47) stitches.

Purl 1 row.

Row 1 (RS) K1, ssk, knit to last 3 stitches, k2tog, k1.
Row 2 Purl.
Row 3 K1, ssk, knit to end.
Row 4 Purl.
Repeat these 4 rows 2 (3, 3, 4, 4) more times—22 (24, 28, 28, 32) stitches.

Shape Cup Top
Row 1 (RS) K1, ssk, knit to last 3 stitches, k2tog, k1.
Row 2 Purl.

Repeat these 2 rows 6 (7, 9, 9, 11) more times—8 stitches.

Work even in stockinette stitch for 12 rows.

Shape Neck Band
Decrease 1 stitch at the beginning of the next 2 rows—6 stitches.

Work even in stockinette stitch for 8¼ (8½, 8¾, 8¾, 9¼)" (21 [21.5, 22, 22, 23.5]cm). Bind off.

With right side facing, join yarn, and single crochet around the sides and end of the 6-stitch band.

Right Cup

Cast on 45 (50, 55, 60, 65) stitches.

Row 1 (RS) K1, ssk, knit to end.
Rows 2–4 Work in stockinette stitch.

Repeat these 4 rows 5 (5, 5, 6, 6) more times—39 (44, 49, 53, 58) stitches remain.

Knit 1 row.

Shape Armhole
Bind off 8 (8, 9, 10, 11) stitches at the beginning of the next wrong-side row for underarm—31 (36, 40, 43, 47) stitches remain.

Row 1 (RS) K1, ssk, knit to last 3 stitches, k2tog, k1.
Row 2 Purl.
Row 3 Knit to last 3 stitches, k2tog, k1.
Row 4 Purl.
Repeat these 4 rows 2 (3, 3, 4, 4) more times—22 (24, 28, 28, 32) stitches remain.

Shape Cup Top
Row 1 (RS) K1, ssk, knit to last 3 stitches, k2tog, k1.
Row 2 Purl.

Repeat these 2 rows 6 (7, 9, 9, 11) more times—8 stitches.

Work even in stockinette stitch for 12 rows.

Shape Neck Band

Decrease 1 stitch at the beginning of the next 2 rows—6 stitches.

Work even in stockinette stitch for 8¼ (8½, 8¾, 8¾, 9¼)" (21 [21.5, 22, 22, 23.5]cm). Bind off.

With right side facing, join yarn and single crochet around the sides and end of the 6-stitch band.

Back Inset

Cast on 50 (55, 60, 65, 70) stitches. Work in stockinette stitch for ¾" (2cm), ending with a wrong-side row.

Purl 1 row on the right side for turning ridge.

Work in stockinette stitch for 3¼ (3¼, 3¼, 3¾, 3¾)" (8 [8, 8, 9.5, 9.5]cm) from turning ridge, ending with a wrong-side row.

If you are not already working on circular needles, slip stitches to the circular needle and cast on 50 (55, 60, 65, 70) stitches at the beginning of the row. Place marker, and join for working in the round, being careful not to twist stitches—100 (110, 120, 130, 140) stitches.

Work in stockinette stitch for 3½" (9cm).

Body

Set-up Round *Knit 10 (11, 12, 13, 14) stitches, place marker; repeat from * to end 9 times more (the last marker will already be in place at the beginning of the round).

Round 1 *Knit to 1 stitch before marker,

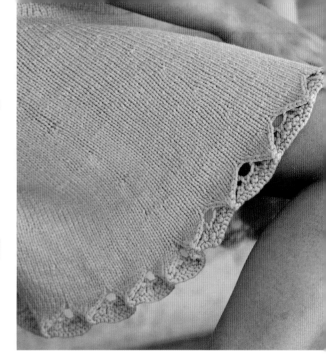

increase in the next stitch; repeat from * to end 9 times more.

Rounds 2–11 Knit.

Repeat these 11 rounds 11 more times—220 (230, 240, 250, 260) stitches total; 22 (23, 24, 25, 26) stitches in each section between markers.

Increase 5 (4, 3, 2, 1) stitches evenly spaced on next round—225 (234, 243, 252, 261) stitches.

Scallop Edging

Beginning with Round 1, work 8 rounds of the Scalloped Edging Pattern.

Bind off.

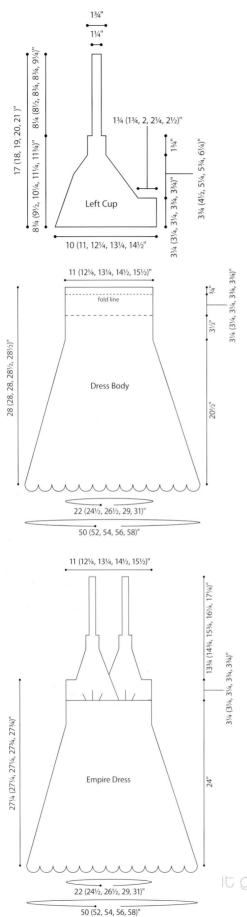

Left Cup

1¾"
1¼"

8¼ (8½, 8¾, 8¾, 9¼)"

17 (18, 19, 20, 21)"

8¾ (9½, 10¼, 11¼, 11¾)"

1¾ (1¾, 2, 2¼, 2½)"

1¾"

3¾ (4½, 5¼, 5¾, 6¼)"

3¼ (3¼, 3¼, 3¾, 3¾)"

10 (11, 12¼, 13¼, 14½"

Dress Body

11 (12¼, 13¼, 14½, 15½)"

fold line

¾"

3½"

3¼ (3¼, 3¼, 3¾, 3¾)"

28 (28, 28, 28½, 28½)"

20½"

22 (24½, 26½, 29, 31)"

50 (52, 54, 56, 58)"

Empire Dress

11 (12¼, 13¼, 14½, 15½)"

13¾ (14¾, 15¾, 16¼, 17¼)"

3¼ (3¼, 3¼, 3¾, 3¾)"

27¼ (27¼, 27¼, 27¾, 27¾)"

24"

22 (24½, 26½, 29, 31)"

50 (52, 54, 56, 58)"

Finishing

Measure 3" (7.5cm) in from both sides of Left Cup, and place pins. Using the yarn needle and matching yarn, sew a running stitch to gather the material between the pins to measure 1½ (2, 2½, 3, 3½)" (4 [5, 6.5, 7.5, 9]cm); the cup should measure 7½ (8, 8½, 9, 9½)" (19 [20.5, 21.5, 23, 24]cm) at the bottom edge. Fasten with a knot on the wrong side to secure the gathers. Repeat to gather the Right Cup.

Using the yarn needle and matching yarn, sew the sides of the Back Inset to the sides of the 2 cups. Sew the cast-on edge of the Dress Body halfway across the cast-on edge of the cups on both sides, ensuring that the rows line up properly. The center of the body and cups are unsewn. Try on the garment to check fit. Continue seaming across Left Cup first. The Right Cup will overlap the left by approximately 3" (7.5cm) at the center of the body. Continue sewing across the Right Cup, working 1 row below the Left Cup where they overlap.

Fold the casing of the Back Inset to the wrong side at the turning ridge. Using a yarn needle and matching yarn, whipstitch the cast-on edge to the wrong side, leaving both ends open. Insert elastic through the casing, pull to fit, and pin it in place. With a sewing needle and thread, sew both ends of elastic in place on the fabric, and cut off any excess elastic.

Weave in ends. Hand wash in cool water. Wring and blot to remove excess water, and dry flat.

Lining and Bra Cup Inserts (Optional)
Cut lining fabric to the appropriate size: the size of the bra cup plus an extra ½" (13mm) of ease all around (for the bra cup to slip inside) and a ¼" (6mm) seam allowance. Fold under seam allowance, and with the sewing needle and thread, tack the lining to the wrong side of each knitted cup, leaving the bottom edge open to insert the bra cup insert. Insert the bra cups, and sew the bottom edges closed.

cropped leggings

Skill Level

Intermediate

Sizes

XS (S, M, L, XL)

Finished Measurements

Hip Circumference: 31 (33, 37, 41, 43)"
(78.5 [84, 94, 104, 109]cm)
Inseam Length: 22 (22½, 22½, 23½, 24½)"
(56 [57, 57, 59.5, 62]cm)

Yarn

- 7 (8, 9, 10, 11) skeins Crystal Palace
  Yarns Panda Cotton, 55% bamboo,
  24% cotton, 21% elastic nylon, 1¾ oz
  (50g), 170 yd (156m), #9598 Jet Black,
  2 fine

Needles and Notions

- US size 4 (3.5mm) double-pointed
  needles, or size needed to obtain
  gauge
- or US size 4 (3.5mm) circular needle,
  40" (101.5cm) long, or size needed to
  obtain gauge
- US size 4 (3.5mm) circular needle, 16"
  (40.5cm) long, or size needed to
  obtain gauge (optional)
- US size 4 (3.5mm) circular needle, 24"
  (61cm) long, or size needed to obtain
  gauge
- Stitch markers
- Stitch holders
- Yarn needle
- 1 yd elastic waistband, ¾" (2cm) wide
- Sewing needle and thread

You won't believe how comfortable knitted leggings are, and if you're worried about stiffness or coverage, don't be. These leggings are made with an easy-care yarn in a bamboo, cotton, and elastic blend that is unbelievably soft and stretchy. Like my other pants patterns, the Cropped Leggings are knit in the round, with special details like a fake seam at the inside of each leg and a totally customizable low elastic waistband to accommodate your body shape.

Gauge

28 stitches and 40 rounds = 4" (10cm) in stockinette stitch when worked in the round. Adjust needle size as necessary to obtain correct gauge.

Notes

1. Check your gauge carefully. Leggings are designed to fit snugly but without pulling the fabric open. To ensure a proper fit in both length and width, try on the leggings at the calf, knee, and thigh as you knit. Reassess your gauge and sizing choice accordingly.

2. The increase stitches form an inseam on each leg, and care must be taken to ensure that they line up vertically. Place a stitch marker before the center stitch of each set of increases to aid in alignment and counting. Evenly graduated increases along the length of the Leg are the key to achieving snug-fitting leggings with maximum coverage.

3. Short rows (page 139) are used to add some fullness to the back of the leggings. Each short row is actually 2 partial rows (Wrap and Turn, page 139) sandwiched between 4 full rounds (described in Steps 1 and 2). Each time you work Steps 1 and 2, you add about ¼" (6mm) in height to the back.

By repeating Steps 1 and 2, you can add as many inches as you like.

4. To adjust the length of the pants, slip leg stitches to waste yarn and try them on to determine how many more inches to work. Return the stitches to the needle, and work as many rows as desired until Join Legs.

Leg (Make 2)

With double-pointed needles or the longest circular (page 138 for Magic Loop), cast on 68 (68, 76, 84, 88) stitches. Place marker, and join for working in the round, being careful not to twist the stitches. Work in k2, p2 rib for ¾" (2cm).

Change to stockinette stitch.

Shape Leg
*Work 7 (6, 6, 5, 5) rounds in stockinette stitch.

Increase Round Starting just before marker, M1R, slip marker, k1, M1L, knit to end.

Repeat from * to end 24 (28, 29, 34, 36) more times until 118 (126, 136, 154, 162) stitches remain.

Work even in stockinette stitch until piece measures 22 (22½, 22½, 23½, 24½)" (56 [57, 57, 59.5, 62]cm) or the desired length from the cast-on edge (see customization instructions in Notes, page 66). Switch to the shortest circular needles (optional) when the circumference of the leg allows.

On the last round, knit to 4 (4, 6, 7, 8) stitches before the marker, work (M1, k1) 9 (10, 14, 15, 17) times to increase for leg join—127 (136, 150, 169, 179) stitches total.

Slip all stitches to a stitch holder.

Join Legs

With faux inseam centered, make leg join by slipping 18 (20, 20, 25, 28) stitches from each Leg onto a stitch holder. These stitches will be joined together later using the Three-Needle Bind-off.

Hold Legs together at the inseam stitches, with right sides facing. With long circular needle, knit the remaining stitches from both Legs, and join for working in the round—218 (232, 260, 288, 302) stitches. Work in stockinette stitch for 2 (2, 3, 4, 5)" (5 [5, 7.5, 10, 12.5]cm).

Divide stitches in half, and place stitch markers at sides of hips so that 109 (116, 130, 144, 151) stitches are in the front and 109 (116, 130, 144, 151) stitches are in the back. Use different colored stitch markers to designate the first marker as Marker 1 and the second as Marker 2.

Short Row Shaping
Short rows are worked flat across the back stitches in stockinette stitch between Markers 1 and 2. The front stitches wait on the needle while short rows are worked, then all hip stitches are worked in the round for 4 rounds between each set of short rows.

Step 1: Knit to 1 stitch before Marker 2. Wrap next stitch, turn work, and purl back to 1 stitch before Marker 1. Wrap and turn.

it girl style secret

Wear the Cropped Leggings with a long tunic top and heels, ballet flats, or canvas sneakers—or if you're a country girl, Wellingtons or cowboy boots.

Step 2: Return to working in the round across the back stitches (between Markers 1 and 2), and continue around entire hip circumference, picking up the wraps and working them together with the stitches that they wrap as you pass them. Work 3 more rounds in stockinette stitch, ending at Marker 1.

Repeat Steps 1 and 2, each time working to 3 stitches before the previous wrapped stitch, until 6 stitches have been wrapped at each side.

Work even in stockinette stitch until the back measures 8½ (8½, 9½, 10½, 11½)" (21.5 [21.5, 24, 26.5, 29]cm) from the leg join.

Purl 1 round on the right side for a turning ridge. Work in stockinette stitch for 1" (2.5cm). Bind off loosely.

Finishing

Fold the waistband to the wrong side of the garment at the turning ridge. Using a yarn needle and matching yarn, whipstitch the bound-off edge to the wrong side, leaving an opening large enough to slide in the waistband elastic; do not break yarn. Cut elastic 1" (2.5cm) longer than your waist measurement. Feed the elastic through the casing, pulling out both ends. Overlap the elastic ends by 1" (2.5cm), and sew them together with a sewing needle and thread. Slide the elastic back into the casing, and sew the casing closed with the yarn needle and yarn.

Three-Needle Bind-off

With the wrong side facing, pick up and knit 1 stitch from the body of the garment, slip 18 (20, 20, 25, 28) stitches from 1 crotch stitch holder onto the needle, and pick up and knit 1 stitch from the body of the garment—20 (22, 22, 27, 30) stitches total.

Repeat for the second set of crotch stitches, picking up and knitting 1 stitch from pants at the beginning, slipping stitches onto a second needle, and knitting 1 stitch from pants at the end. Hold the pieces with right sides facing, and using a third needle, knit together 1 stitch each from front and back needles. Repeat, then bind off the first stitch. Continue to bind off all the crotch stitches in this manner.

Weave in ends. Hand wash or machine wash with cool water on gentle cycle. Wring and blot to remove excess water, and dry flat.

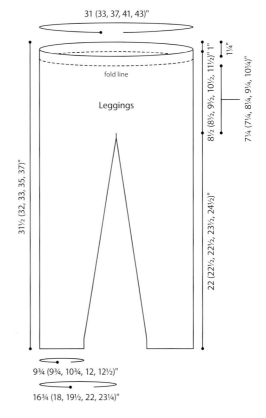

31 (33, 37, 41, 43)"

fold line

Leggings

8½ (8½, 9½, 10½, 11½)" 1"

1¼"

7¼ (7¼, 8¼, 9¼, 10¼)"

31½ (32, 33, 35, 37)"

22 (22½, 22½, 23½, 24½)"

9¾ (9¾, 10¾, 12, 12½)"

16¾ (18, 19½, 22, 23¼)"

aussie
boots

Skill Level

Intermediate

Sizes

XS (S, M, L, XL)
Women's US size 4–5 (6–7, 8–9, 10–11, 12)
[Men's US size 10])

Finished Measurements

Width x Length (after felting): 3¾ (3¾, 4¼,
4¼, 4¾)" (9.5 [9.5, 11, 11, 12]cm) x 8½ (9,
9½, 10, 11)" (21.5 [23, 24, 25.5, 28]cm)

Yarn

- 3 skeins Patons Classic Merino Wool,
  100% wool, 3½ oz (100g), 223 yd
  (205m), #00201 Winter White,
  4 medium

Needles and Notions

- US size 10.5 (6.5mm) knitting needles,
  or size needed to obtain gauge
- US size 10.5 (6.5mm) circular needle,
  16" (40.5cm) long, or size needed to
  obtain gauge
- Stitch marker
- Yarn needle
- Pins
- Simple Shoemaking "Soles with an
  Edge" (for outdoor wear)
- or Fiber Trends® Suede Slipper Soles
  (for indoor wear only)
- Utility knife
- 1 Crazy Crow Rabbit Skin, Large,
  Prime, white or ½ yd (0.5m) faux fur
- Sewing needle and strong thread

These boots are totally hot. Did you ever think
you could knit footwear sturdy enough to wear
to work, to school, or out shopping? Super
simple knitting makes the Aussie Boots a great
project, but the felting, fur trim, and soles
make these boots special. A luxurious (yet
inexpensive) rabbit fur or faux fur trims the cuffs.
Purchased soles, attached with simple stitching,
make the boots perfect for walking anywhere.

Gauge

14 stitches and 20 rows = 4" (10cm) in stockinette stitch when worked flat, before felting.

Adjust needle size as necessary to obtain correct gauge.

Notes

1. Sole is worked back and forth in rows, from the heel to the toe. The cast-on edge is folded in half to create a heel, and the toe is gathered.
2. The Instep is worked separately and fitted into the Sole.
3. Stitches are picked up around the Sole and Instep and worked in the round up the Leg.
4. Purchased soles are attached to the Aussie Boot after felting.

Sole (Make 2)

Cast on 32 (32, 34, 34, 36) stitches. Work in stockinette stitch for 7¾ (8½, 9, 9¾, 10)" (19.5 [21.5, 23, 25, 25.5]cm).

Shape Toe
Row 1 K1, ssk, knit to last 3 stitches, k2tog, k1.
Rows 2–6 Work in stockinette stitch.
Repeat these 6 rows 2 more times—26 (26, 28, 28, 30) stitches.

Row 1 K1, ssk, knit to last 3 stitches, k2tog, k1.
Rows 2–4 Work in stockinette stitch.
Repeat these 4 rows 0 (0, 1, 1, 2) times more—24 stitches.

Row 1 K1, ssk, knit to last 3 stitches, k2tog, k1.
Row 2 Purl.

Repeat these 2 rows once more—20 stitches.

Row 1 K1, sssk, knit to last 4 stitches, k3tog, k1—16 stitches.
Row 2 P1, p3tog, purl to last 4 stitches, sssp, p1—12 stitches.
Row 3 K1, ssk, knit to last 3 stitches, k2tog, k1—10 stitches.
Row 4 P1, p2tog, purl to last 3 stitches, ssp, p1—8 stitches.
Row 5 K1, sssk, k3tog, k1—4 stitches.

Bind off remaining stitches purlwise.

Instep (Make 2)

Cast on 16 (16, 18, 18, 20) stitches with waste yarn. Switch to pattern yarn, and work in stockinette stitch for 4½ (5, 5, 5½, 5 ½)" (11.5 [12.5, 12.5, 14, 14]cm).

Shape Toe
Row 1 K1, ssk, knit to last 3 stitches, k2tog, k1.
Rows 2–4 Work in stockinette stitch.

Repeat these 4 rows 0 (0, 1, 1, 2) more times—14 stitches.

Row 1 K1, ssk, knit to last 3 stitches, k2tog, k1—12 stitches.
Row 2 Purl.
Row 3 K1, sssk, knit to last 4 stitches, k3tog, k1—8 stitches.
Row 4 Purl.
Row 5 K1, sssk, k3tog, k1—4 stitches.

Bind off remaining stitches purlwise.

Shape Arch
Pick up cast-on stitches at beginning of Instep and cut waste yarn—16 (16, 18, 18, 20) stitches.

Row 1 (RS) Knit 7 stitches, join a second ball of yarn and bind off 2 (2, 4, 4, 6) stitches loosely, knit 7 stitches—14 stitches.

Work both sides of the arch at the same time with separate balls of yarn.

Row 2 P4, sssp, p3tog, p4—10 stitches.
Row 3 K2, k3tog, sssk, k2—6 stitches.
Row 4 P1, ssp, p2tog, p1—4 stitches.

Bind off remaining stitches.

Join Sole to Instep

Cut 1 yd (91cm) of yarn, and work a running stitch around the toe of the Sole, beginning and ending on either side at first decrease row of toe shaping. Pull the yarn to gather the end of the Sole to measure 13 (13, 14, 14, 15)" (33 [33, 35.5, 35.5, 38]cm). Work your fingers across the gathers to even them out, concentrating the most gathers at the toe and gradually tapering out after 2" (5cm) on each side until the side of the foot is straight.

With right sides together, fit the Instep into the gathered toe of the Sole and pin in place. The gathered stitches along the toe will make a ridge at the join to the Instep. Whipstitch the Instep and Sole together along length of Instep, leaving the outside edge of the Sole unsewn.

Fold the remaining part of the Sole in half lengthwise. Whipstitch the cast-on edge together, beginning at the top corners and ending 1½" (4cm) from the bottom of the folded edge. Fold the remaining open part up, and sew to the outside of the end of the heel.

Leg

With a circular needle, pick up and knit 54 (56, 60, 62, 66) stitches evenly around the foot opening. To prevent holes, pick up the stitches from under both loops of the stitches along the edge. Place a marker and join for working in the round, being careful not to twist the stitches. Work in stockinette stitch for 16" (40.5cm). Bind off loosely.

Finishing

Weave in ends. Felt to finished measurements following instructions in the Felting sidebar (page 49). To felt any remaining rough spots at joins (e.g., of the Sole or Instep to Leg or along the gathered toe), move boots to a sink. Wearing rubber gloves to protect your hands, pour very hot water on each rough spot. Rub a bar of soap over the spot, and rub the wool with your fingers or rough towel, or simply rub

the boots together. Add more hot water to the spot, rub on more soap, and continue to rub until the roughness disappears. Rinse boots thoroughly, and wring carefully to remove excess water. Lay the boots between 2 clean towels and press to blot more water, taking care not to press creases into the felted fabric.

Try on the boots. If any part feels too tight, remove the boot and push and pull those tight areas until they stretch to fit.

The Aussie Boots should fit snugly to start, because they will stretch with wear. Stuff the boots with plastic bags to block, and set them aside to dry for several days.

Fur Trim

Rabbit Trim: Using the utility knife on a cutting board or mat, cut the pelt in half lengthwise into 2 pieces.

Faux Fur: Decide on desired width of your fur trim, and add 1" (2.5cm) for a seam allowance. Measure around the top edge of the Leg for the length measurement, and add ½" (13mm) seam allowance. Using the utility knife on a cutting board or mat, cut 2 pieces of faux fur to fit around the tops of the boots. Cut 1 long edge of each piece unevenly to resemble a natural pelt.

For Both Trims: With wrong sides together, position 1" (2.5cm) of a straight edge of a trim piece around the inside of a boot. Overlap the short edges, and sew in place with a sewing needle and strong thread. The uneven edge of the fur trim will fold over the top edge of the boot. Make several loose stitches around the top edge of the outside of the boot to keep the fur piece secured.

Repeat for the other boot.

Attach Sole

Outdoor Soles: To make regular boots for street wear, order outdoor soles from Simple Shoemaking (page 142), then follow the manufacturer's guidelines for attaching to the boot. You also can mail the boots to the outdoor sole manufacturer and have the soles sewn on for you.

Indoor Soles: If you want to wear your felted footwear as house slippers, sew on Fiber Trends® suede slipper soles according to the manufacturer's instructions.

····· it girl style secret

Wear the Aussie Boots with shorts, a miniskirt, or jeans.

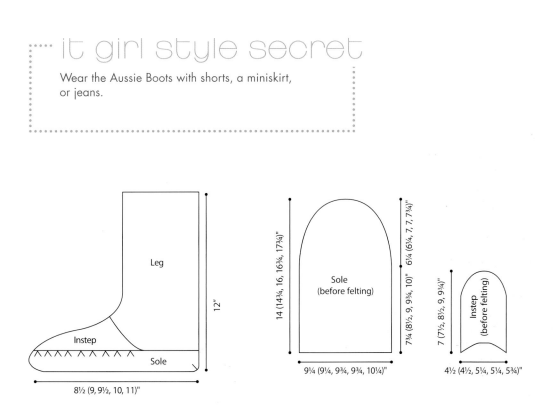

Leg

Instep

Sole

12"

8½ (9, 9½, 10, 11)"

14 (14¾, 16, 16¾, 17¾)"

Sole
(before felting)

6¼ (6¼, 7, 7, 7¾)"

7¾ (8½, 9, 9¾, 10)"

9¼ (9¼, 9¾, 9¾, 10¼)"

7 (7½, 8½, 9, 9¾)"

Instep
(before felting)

4½ (4½, 5¼, 5¼, 5¾)"

lacy camisole

Skill Level

Easy

Sizes

XS (S, M, L, XL)

Finished Measurements

Bust Circumference: 30 (32, 36, 40, 42)"
(76 [81, 91, 101.5, 106.5]cm)
Length (excluding straps): 17½ (17¾, 18½,
19¼, 19½)" (44.5 [45, 47, 49, 49.5]cm)

Yarn

- 2 (2, 2, 3, 3) skeins Southwest Trading
  Company Bamboo, 100% bamboo, 3½
  oz (100g), 250 yd (229m), #402
  Magenta, (3) light

Needles and Notions

- US size 5 (3.75mm) circular needle, 24"
  (60cm) long, or size needed to obtain
  gauge
- US size F-5 (3.75mm) crochet hook
- Stitch markers
- Yarn needle
- 1 yd (1m) satin ribbon, ⅜" (10mm)
  wide, white
- Aleene's® Fabric Fusion™ Permanent
  Dry Cleanable Fabric Adhesive™
- Sewing needle and white thread
- 2 plastic bra strap slides, ½" (13mm),
  clear
- 2 plastic bra strap rings, ½" (13mm),
  clear
- 3 yd (2.75m) M&J Trimming Victorian
  Fine Lace, ⅝" (16mm) wide, white
- 1 yd (91cm) elastic thread, 3mm

I love the way a camisole can be so dainty
and feminine but a little flirty, too. Peeking from
under a jacket or sweater, a camisole shows
your soft side, even if you're wearing a biker
jacket. This one is worked up in an amazing
bamboo yarn and embellished with ribbons
and lingerie lace.

Gauge

24 stitches and 36 rounds = 4" (10cm) in stockinette
stitch when worked in the round. Adjust needle size as
necessary to obtain correct gauge.

Notes

1. The split hems are first worked separately, back and
forth in rows, then are joined to work in the round to
form the Body of the camisole.
2. Use a different colored stitch marker for the
beginning of the round.

Abbreviations

Ssk: Slip 1 stitch knitwise, slip the next stitch knitwise,
then knit the 2 slipped stitches together through the
backs of their loops.
Ssp: Slip 1 stitch knitwise, slip the next stitch knitwise,
then purl the 2 slipped stitches together through the
backs of their loops.

Split Hem (Make 2)

Cast on 90 (96, 108, 120, 126) stitches. Starting with a
purl row, work 5 rows in stockinette stitch. Purl 1 row
to create a turning ridge. Work even in stockinette
stitch for 3" (7.5cm), ending with a wrong-side row.
Break the yarn, and leave stitches on the needle for
joining later.

Body

With right side facing, place marker for beginning of the round, knit across the stitches of first Hem piece, place marker for side edge, knit across stitches of second Hem piece. Join for working in the round—180 (192, 216, 240, 252) stitches.

Shape Waist
Round 1 *Ssk, knit to 3 stitches before next marker, k2tog, k1; repeat from * to end once.
Rounds 2–6 Knit.

Repeat these 6 rounds 2 more times—168 (180, 204, 228, 240) stitches.

Knit 4 rounds.

Round 1 *M1, knit to 1 stitch before next marker, M1, k1; repeat from * to end once.
Rounds 2–6 Knit.

Repeat these 6 rounds 2 more times—180 (192, 216, 240, 252) stitches.

Work even in stockinette stitch until piece measures 13" (33cm) from the turning ridge.

Divide for Back and Front
Next Round Bind off 90 (96, 108, 120, 126) stitches for the Back, k44 (47, 53, 59, 62) for the Left Cup, bind off 2 stitches, k44 (47, 53, 59, 62) for the Right Cup.

Right Cup

Work back and forth on the 44 (47, 53, 59, 62) stitches just knit.

Row 1 (WS) Purl.
Row 2 Ssk, knit to last 2 stitches, k2tog.

Repeat these 2 rows 2 more times—38 (41, 47, 53, 56) stitches.

Row 1 (WS) P2tog, purl to last 2 stitches, ssp.
Row 2 Ssk, knit to last 2 stitches, k2tog.

Repeat these 2 rows 17 (18, 21, 24, 26) more times—2 (3, 3, 3, 2) stitches. Bind off.

Left Cup

With wrong side facing, join yarn at center of the Front and work back and forth on the 44 (47, 53, 59, 62) stitches of Left Cup.

Row 1 (WS) Purl.
Row 2 Ssk, knit to last 2 stitches, k2tog.

Repeat these 2 rows 2 more times—38 (41, 47, 53, 56) stitches.

Row 1 (WS) P2tog, purl to last 2 stitches, ssp.
Row 2 Ssk, knit to last 2 stitches, k2tog.

Repeat these 2 rows 17 (18, 21, 24, 26) more times—2 (3, 3, 3, 2) stitches. Bind off.

---

it girl style secret

Don't be afraid to let this little jewel show. Wear the Lacy Camisole with your favorite boot-cut jeans, a slim skirt and a tailored jacket, or the matching Flirty Short Skirt (page 23).

Finishing

Fold up hem at turning ridge. Using yarn needle and matching yarn, whipstitch hem to the wrong side.

With the right side facing, join yarn at the underarm edge, and single crochet evenly around entire top edge of the Lacy Camisole.

Weave in ends. Hand wash with cool water. Wring and blot to remove excess water, and dry flat.

Straps

Cut 2 lengths of ribbon 5" (12.5cm) long and 2 lengths of ribbon 18" (45.5cm) long. Seal all cut ends of ribbon with Fabric Fusion™ or clear glue, and allow them to dry.

Fold over both ends of each ribbon by ½" (13mm), and use a sewing needle and thread to secure. Tack 1 end of long ribbon to the wrong side the top point of each cup.

Lay the camisole with the front down on a table with the right side facing, and thread the ribbon through the bra slides. Place the bra slides 9" (23cm) from the tacked end of ribbon. Next, thread the ribbon through the rings and place the rings 2½" (6.5cm) from slide. Bring the end of the ribbon back through the slide, and secure it on the wrong side.

Flip over garment to work on the inside of the Back. Thread a shorter ribbon through a ring and fold in half to create a tab to hold the ring, and connect it to a long strap. Tack the folded edges of the short ribbon tabs to the wrong side at the top edge of the Back, 5½" (14cm) in from each side.

Cut lace trim to fit around top and bottom edges of the camisole, and pin it in place. Tack the lace trim around the crochet edge with a sewing needle and thread.

With a yarn needle, thread 3mm elastic thread through the inside of the crochet edge along the top of the Back, and pull to fit. Secure ends with thread or glue.

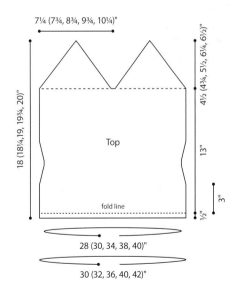

designer carryall

Skill Level

Easy

Size

One size

Finished Measurements

Height x Width x Depth (before felting): 19" (48.5cm) x12½" (32cm) x 6" (15cm) Height x Width x Depth (after felting): 12" (30.5cm) x11" (28cm) wide x 5" (12.5cm)

Yarn

▨ 7 skeins Nashua Handknits Creative Focus Worsted, 75% wool, 25% alpaca, 3½ oz (100g), 220 yd (201m), #9130 Fuchsia, (4) medium

Needles and Notions

▨ US size 10.5 (6.5mm) knitting needle, or size needed to obtain gauge
▨ 1 pair Grayson E Long Rolled Leather Handles with Buckles, 18½" (47cm), Hot Pink
▨ 1 pair Grayson E Leather Base Cups, 5½" (14cm) x 5" (12.5cm), Hot Pink
▨ 2 skeins Size 5 Anchor Pearl Mercerized Cotton (5g), #89 Dark Orchid
▨ Yarn needle
▨ Dressmaker's pencil

Jeweled Keychain Notions (Optional)

▨ Clear Accu-Flex® Beading Wire, 49-strand, 0.024-inch diameter
▨ 1 jump ring, 20.5 gauge, 6mm round, sterling silver

This bag really is meant to carry all of your stuff. Use it for sleepovers, day trips to the country, or shopping around town. Easy to knit in garter stitch on big needles, this designer-style carryall is a fun project that beginner and advanced knitters alike can whip up in no time. Just knit the simple rectangular panels, seam, and felt. The fun part is adding special leather handles and base cups that make the bag look decidedly not homemade. An optional cute jeweled keychain with sterling silver square alphabet beads is the perfect customization for the knitter with crafty skills.

▨ 1 round lobster claw clasp, medium, sterling silver
▨ 2 crimps, cut tube, 3mm x 2mm, sterling silver
▨ 1 each alphabet cube bead, 5.5mm, letters P, H, O, E, N, I, and X (or your name), sterling silver
▨ 3 Swarovski® Crystal Beads Round Faceted, 6mm, Tanzanite
▨ 8 Swarovski® Crystal Beads Bicone Faceted, 6mm, Amethyst
▨ 2 Swarovski® Crystal Beads Bicone Faceted, 6mm, Capri Blue
▨ 2 Swarovski® Crystal Beads Rondelle Faceted, 6mm, Caribbean Blue Opal
▨ 4 Swarovski® Crystal Beads Round Faceted, 10mm, Crystal AB
▨ 2 Swarovski® Crystal Beads Round Faceted, 8mm, Crystal AB
▨ Chain-nose pliers

Gauge

15 stitches and 26 rows = 4" (10cm) in garter stitch when worked flat, with 2 strands of yarn held together, before felting. Adjust needle size as necessary to obtain correct gauge.

> It's a bag—wear it with everything! What's more,
> the optional jeweled personalized key chain also
> can be worn as a bracelet.

Notes

1. The bag is knit with 2 strands of yarn held together throughout the pattern.
2. The bag is worked in back and forth in rows in 5 pieces, which are then sewn together and felted. Purchased straps and base cup are sewn on.

Sides (Make 2)

Cast on 47 stitches. Work in garter stitch for 19" (48.5cm). Bind off.

Ends (Make 2)

Cast on 22 stitches. Work in garter stitch for 19" (48.5cm). Bind off.

Bottom

Cast on 47 stitches. Work in garter stitch for 6" (15cm). Bind off.

Finishing

Using yarn needle and matching yarn, whipstitch the pieces together. Weave in ends.

Following the instructions on felting (page 49), felt the bag to the finished measurements. Keep checking the bag often to control the amount of felting. When it has reached the correct size, remove the bag from the washer and rinse it in cold water until the water runs clear. Squeeze out excess water, and blot the felted project between clean dry towels. Pull the bag into shape while it is still wet.

To block the bag while it's drying, find a square shape to put in the bottom of the bag to help it hold its shape. Any combination of cereal boxes, books, and other rectangular or square shapes can be used—slip a plastic grocery bag over them first to keep them dry. Fill the bag with as many items as needed to make the bottom and sides conform to the specified dimensions, and set aside the purse to dry.

Attach Hardware

Using a dressmaker's pencil, mark the bag for the correct placement of the base cups. They are placed in the corners between the bottom and the side panels of the bag. Check the placement of the base cups for evenness and symmetry (and this can be a bit tricky, because felting may make your perfectly rectangular knit a bit uneven or lopsided). Using a sewing needle and a double strand of pearl cotton, sew the base cups to the bag with a backstitch. Using a dressmaker's pencil, mark the position of the handles, 2" (5cm) from the outside edges of the bag and 5" (12.5cm) from the top. Again, don't worry too much about exact measurements, because your bag may not be perfectly rectangular. Eyeball the placement to make sure it all looks even. Using a double strand of pearl cotton, sew on the handles.

Jeweled Keychain (Optional)

Cut beading wire to 8" (20.5cm), and follow instructions on jewelry-making box (page 81) for making the Jeweled Keychain.

String the beads in this order: Tanzanite bead, Amethyst bicone, Crystal AB 8mm, Caribbean Blue Opal rondelle, Tanzanite bead, Crystal AB

10mm, Capri Blue bicone, Crystal AB 10mm, P alphabet bead, Amethyst bicone, H alphabet bead, Amethyst bicone, O alphabet bead, Amethyst bicone, E alphabet bead, Amethyst bicone, N alphabet bead, Amethyst bicone, I alphabet bead, Amethyst bicone, X alphabet bead, Crystal AB 8mm, Capri Blue bicone, Crystal AB 10mm, Tanzanite bead, Caribbean Blue Opal rondelle, Crystal AB 10mm, Amethyst bicone.

Attach the jeweled keychain to the handle of your purse.

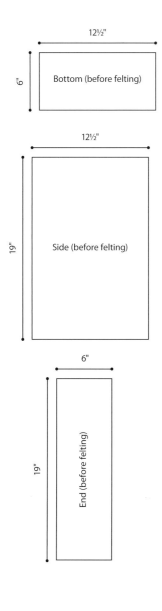

12½"

6" Bottom (before felting)

12½"

19" Side (before felting)

6"

19" End (before felting)

jewelry making

1. Cut beading wire to the length specified in pattern.
2. Slide a crimp tube and a jump ring onto 1 end.
3. Tuck the wire into the crimp tube, and slide the jump ring and crimp tube to the end of the wire, leaving a ⅛" (3mm) loop in the beading wire between the crimp tube and the jump ring.
4. With chain-nose pliers, squeeze the crimp tube.
5. String beads onto the wire in the order indicated in the pattern.
6. Slide on a second crimp tube and the clasp.
7. Tuck the end of wire into the crimp tube and through the last bead.
8. Cut the wire flush with the bead and push against the bead to allow wire end to slip inside of the bead to hide.
9. Crimp the tube with the chain-nose pliers.

play
days

These are some of the quickest knitting projects you'll find. Not only are the design details totally hot, but the knitting is easy and fun. Whip up an outfit during the week, and you'll have the cutest clothes for your sun-drenched weekend. Whether you're planning a trip to a fabulous resort or just popping into a summer beach cottage with a few friends, you'll definitely want to have these garments with you.

workout
top

Skill Level

Easy

Sizes

XS (S, M, L, XL)

Finished Measurements

Bust Circumference: 25¼ (27, 30¼, 33½, 35¼)" (64 [68.5, 77, 85, 89.5]cm)
Length (excluding straps): 7½ (7½, 8¼, 9, 9)" (19 [19, 21, 23, 23]cm)

Yarn

▦ 2 (2, 3, 3, 4) balls Crystal Palace Yarns Bamboozle, 55% bamboo, 24% cotton, 21% elastic nylon, 1¾ oz (50g), 90 yd (82m), #8211 Fuchsia (A), ❹ medium
▦ 1 ball, Crystal Palace Yarns Bamboozle, #2342 Sprite Green (B)

Needles and Notions

▦ US size 5 (3.75mm) knitting needles
▦ US size 8 (5mm) circular needle, 24" (61cm) long, or size needed to obtain gauge
▦ US size F-5 (3.75mm) crochet hook
▦ Stitch markers
▦ Yarn needle

Gauge

19 stitches and 28 rounds = 4" (10cm) in stockinette stitch on US size 8 needles. Adjust needle size as necessary to obtain correct gauge.

Notes

1. The Workout Top is worked in the round from the lower edge to the underarm.

Wear it to the gym, the beach, or yoga class. Knit it up in no time with the super soft, stretchy bamboo-cotton blend yarn (with elastic for plenty of give and coverage). The contrasting slipped stitch trim makes it stand out from typical exercise wear. Circular knitting and minimal seaming and shaping make this project quick and easy.

Stitches are then bound off for the back. The remaining Front stitches are worked back and forth in rows. 2. When binding off stitches, bind off in pattern. Slip the first stitch in each set of bound-off stitches to give a nice finished edge.

Workout Top

With circular needle and A, cast on 120 (128, 144, 160, 168) stitches. Place marker, and join for working in the round, being careful not to twist stitches.

Work 7 rounds in k2, p2 rib.

Change to stockinette stitch and work until piece measures 4 (4, 4½, 5, 5)" (10 [10, 11.5, 12.5, 12.5]cm) from the cast-on edge.

Divide for Front and Back

Bind off 60 (64, 72, 80, 84) stitches for back, then work to end of round. Turn work and purl 1 row.

Front

Working back and forth in rows on the remaining 60 (64, 72, 80, 84) stitches for the Front, bind off 2 stitches at the beginning of the next 4 rows—52 (56, 64, 72, 76) stitches.

Rows 1–2 Work in stockinette stitch.

···· it girl style secret

Wear this cute little top with the Comfy Cotton Pants
(page 41) to a Pilates workout or to the park for a
quick jog. Or, pair it with the Capri Pants (page 57)
at your next beach party.

Row 3 (RS) Ssk, knit to last 2 stitches, k2tog.
Row 4 Purl.

Repeat these 4 rows 2 more times—46 (50, 58,
66, 70) stitches.

Next Row K16 (16, 20, 24, 24), bind off 14 (18,
18, 18, 22) stitches, k16 (16, 20, 24, 24).

Shape Right Neck
Work on the first 16 (16, 20, 24, 24) stitches
only, leaving remaining stitches unworked for
Left Neck.

Row 1 (WS) Purl.
Row 2 Bind off 4 stitches, knit to end.

Repeat these 2 rows 3 (3, 4, 5, 5) more times
until all stitches are bound off.

Shape Left Neck
With right side facing, join yarn at the neck
edge.

Row 1 (WS) Bind off 4 stitches, purl to end.
Row 2 Knit.

Repeat these 2 rows 3 (3, 4, 5, 5) more times
until all stitches are bound off.

Straps (Make 2)

With smaller needles and A, cast on 58 stitches.
Bind off.

Finishing

Sew 1 end of each strap to the wrong side of
the top edge of the Front.

Crochet Trim
Round 1 With A, single crochet around entire
top edge of the Workout Top, including straps.
Round 2 With B, slip stitch in each single
crochet.

Sew the opposite end of each strap to the
wrong side of the top edge of the back.

Weave in ends. Hand wash or machine wash
with cool water on the gentle cycle. Wring and
blot to remove excess water, and dry flat.

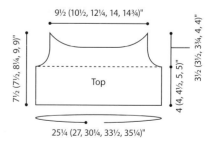

9½ (10½, 12¼, 14, 14¾)"

7½ (7½, 8¼, 9, 9)"

4 (4, 4½, 5, 5)"

3½ (3½, 3¾, 4, 4)"

Top

25¼ (27, 30¼, 33½, 35¼)"

tankini

Skill Level

Intermediate

Sizes

XS (S, M, L, XL)

Finished Measurements

Bust Circumference (Top): 24 (25¾, 29¾, 33¾, 36)" (61 [65.5, 75.5, 85.5, 91]cm) unstretched
Length (Top, excluding straps): 12¼ (12½, 13½, 14½, 15¼)" (31 [32, 34.5, 37, 38.5]cm)
Hip Circumference (Bottom, unstretched): 22 (24, 28, 32, 34)" (56 [61, 71, 81, 86.5]cm)

Yarn

▨ 4 (4, 5, 6, 7) skeins Elle Stretch DK, 90% acrylic, 10% stretch polyester, 1¾ oz (50g), 170 yd (155m), #053 Mid Pink, (❸) light

Needles and Notions

▨ US size 3 (3.25mm) circular needle, 16" (40.5cm) long, or size needed to obtain gauge
▨ US size D-3 (3.25mm) crochet hook
▨ Stitch marker
▨ Stitch holder
▨ Yarn needle
▨ 3 yd (3m) elastic thread (fabric-covered beading cord works), 3mm, pink

Gauge

28 stitches and 38 rows = 4" (10cm) in stockinette stitch. Adjust needle size as necessary to obtain correct gauge.

I found the perfect yarn for this sporty suit. It won't sag when it's wet, which means that it's not coming off in the water. You can knit this bathing suit with the confidence that it will be perfectly functional, with all the little details—a cute keyhole, an easy I-cord halter tie, and 2 x 2 ribbing—it's going to be your summer favorite.

Notes

1. The Top is worked in the round from the lower edge to the underarm. Stitches are then bound off for the Back. The remaining Front stitches are worked back and forth in rows.
2. The Bottom is worked back and forth in rows, in 1 piece from the Front to the Back.

Tankini Top

Cast on 168 (180, 208, 236, 252) stitches. Place marker, and join for working in the round, being careful not to twist stitches.

Work in k2, p2 rib for 2" (5cm). Change to stockinette stitch and work until piece measures 4" (10cm) from the cast-on edge.

Shape Back

Knit to 6 (6, 7, 7, 8) stitches before marker, bind off 12 (12, 14, 16, 16) stitches (removing marker), knit to end of round—156 (168, 194, 220, 236) stitches.

Turn work, and begin working back and forth in rows. Bind off 3 stitches at the beginning of the next 8 (8, 10, 12, 12) rows, then bind off 2 stitches at the beginning of the next 14 (16, 18, 20, 22) rows—104 (112, 128, 144, 156) stitches.

Divide Front (WS) P2tog, purl 48 (52, 60, 68, 74), p2tog—50 (54, 62, 70, 76) stitches. Place remaining 52 (56, 64, 72, 78) stitches on a stitch holder for Left Front.

Right Front

Row 1 (RS) Knit to last 2 stitches, k2tog.

Row 2 P2tog, purl to last 2 stitches, p2tog.

Repeat these 2 rows once more—44 (48, 56, 64, 70) stitches remain.

Row 1 (RS) Knit to last 2 stitches, k2tog.
Row 2 P2tog, purl to end.
Repeat these 2 rows 1 (2, 5, 8, 10) more times—40 (42, 44, 46, 48) stitches remain.

Row 1 Knit.
Row 2 P2tog, purl to end.

Repeat these 2 rows 19 more times—20 (22, 24, 26, 28) stitches remain.

Shape Right Strap Casing

Row 1 Bind off 7 (8, 8, 9, 10) stitches, knit to end—13 (14, 16, 17, 18) stitches.
Row 2 P2tog, purl to end—12 (13, 15, 16, 17) stitches.
Row 3 Bind off 6 (6, 7, 8, 8) stitches, knit to end—6 (7, 8, 8, 9) stitches.
Row 4 P2tog, purl to end—5 (6, 7, 7, 8) stitches.
Bind off remaining stitches.

Left Front

With wrong side facing, slip the 52 (56, 64, 72, 78) stitches from the stitch holder to the needle, and join yarn.

Next Row (WS) P2tog, purl 48 (52, 60, 68, 74), p2tog—50 (54, 62, 70, 76) stitches remain.

Row 1 K2tog, knit to end.
Row 2 P2tog, purl to last 2 stitches, p2tog.

Repeat these 2 rows 2 more times—44 (48, 56, 64, 70) stitches remain.

Row 1 K2tog, knit to end.
Row 2 Purl to last 2 stitches, p2tog.

Repeat these 2 rows 1 (2, 5, 8, 10) more times—40 (42, 44, 46, 48) stitches remain.

Row 1 K2tog, knit to end.
Row 2 Purl.

Repeat these 2 rows 19 more times—20 (22, 24, 26, 28) stitches remain.

Knit 1 row.

Shape Left Strap Casing

Row 1 Bind off 7 (8, 8, 9, 10) stitches, purl to end—13 (14, 16, 17, 18) stitches.
Row 2 k2tog, knit to end—12 (13, 15, 16, 17) stitches.
Row 3 Bind off 6 (6, 7, 8, 8) stitches, purl to end—6 (7, 8, 8, 9) stitches.
Row 4 K2tog, knit to end—5 (6, 7, 7, 8) stitches.
Bind off remaining stitches.

Tankini Bottom

Front

Cast on 66 (74, 88, 102, 108) stitches. Work in stockinette stitch for 4" (10cm), ending with a wrong-side row.

Bind off 10 (10, 12, 14, 14) stitches at the beginning of the next 2 rows—46 (54, 64, 74, 80) stitches.

Row 1 (RS) K1, k3tog through the back loop, knit to last 4 stitches, k3tog, k1.
Row 2 Purl.

Repeat these 2 rows 2 (3, 4, 5, 6) more times—34 (38, 44, 50, 52) stitches remain.

Row 1 (RS) K1, ssk, knit to last 3 stitches, k2tog, k1.
Row 2 Purl.

Repeat these 2 rows 5 (7, 9, 11, 11) more times until 22 (22, 24, 26, 28) stitches remain.

Work even in stockinette stitch until piece measures 7 (7, 8, 9, 10)" (18 [18, 20.5, 23, 25.5]cm) from beginning, ending with a wrong-side row.

Back

Row 1 (RS) K1, M1, knit to last stitch, M1, k1.
Row 2 Purl.

Repeat these 2 rows 25 (28, 32, 37, 40) more times—74 (80, 90, 102, 110) stitches.

Cast on 7 (7, 9, 10, 10) stitches at the end of the next 2 rows—88 (94, 108, 122, 130) stitches total. Work even in stockinette stitch for 4" (10cm). Bind off.

Finishing

Tankini Top
With right side facing, join yarn at underarm of Top and single crochet around the top edges.

Weave elastic cord in and out of crochet trim and around the Top edges, if necessary, to achieve a comfortable fit.

I-Cord
Cast on 3 stitches. *Slide stitches to the other end of needle and knit them, pulling yarn tightly across the back of the work. Do not turn work. Repeat from * to end until the I-cord is 40" (101.5cm) long. Bind off.

Fold the Right Front and Left Front casings by ½" (13mm) to the wrong side of top and whipstitch in place, leaving both ends open. Insert I-cord through both casings.

Tankini Bottom
Sew side seams together.

With right side facing, join yarn at hip opening, and single crochet around the top edges.

Weave elastic cord in and out of crochet trim and around leg openings, if necessary, to achieve a comfortable fit.

Weave in ends. Machine wash in cool water on gentle cycle. Wring and blot to remove excess water, and dry flat.

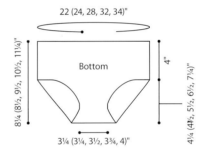

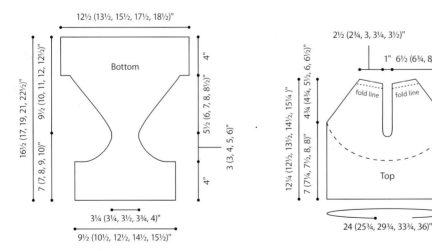

tiny
shorts

Skill Level

Intermediate

Sizes

XS (S, M, L, XL)

Finished Measurements

Hip Circumference: 32 (34, 38, 42, 44)" (81 [86, 96.5, 106.5, 112]cm)
Back Length: 9½ (10, 10½, 11, 11½)" (24 [25.5, 26.5, 28, 29]cm)

Yarn

▒ 4 (5, 6, 6, 7) balls of Crystal Palace Yarns Bamboozle, 55% bamboo, 24% cotton, 21% elastic nylon, 1¾ oz (50g), 90 yd (82m), #0406 Carib Blue, ④ medium

Needles and Notions

▒ US size 8 (5mm) circular needle, 16" (40.5cm) long, or size needed to obtain gauge
▒ US size 8 (5mm) circular needle, 24" (61cm) long, or size needed to obtain gauge
▒ Stitch markers
▒ Stitch holders
▒ Yarn needle
▒ 1½ yd (1.5m) elastic waistband, 1½" (4cm) wide
▒ Sewing needle and thread
▒ 3 yd (3m) satin ribbon, ½" (13mm) wide, blue

Gauge

19 stitches and 28 rounds = 4" (10cm) in stockinette stitch when worked in the round.

Another garment to add to your list of easy-to-knit must-haves, this pair of shorts is long on options and short on tricky techniques. It's just simple circular knitting from the turned cuffs to the drawstring waistband, and customizable short rows to keep that back under wraps.

Adjust needle size as necessary to obtain correct gauge.

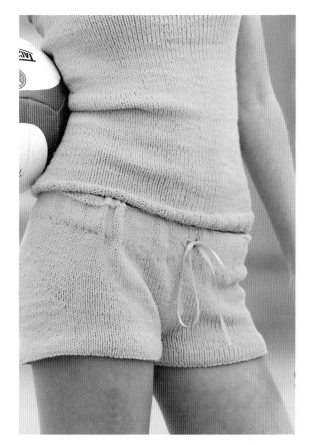

Wear the Tiny Shorts with a T-shirt or a tiny cropped
top, or pull them on over your Tankini (page 87)
for a quick trip to Dairy Queen to get a strawberry
cheesecake Blizzard.

Notes

1. Legs are worked separately in the round and
then joined.
2. Short rows (page 139) are used to add fullness
to the back of the shorts. Each short row is
actually 2 partial rows (Wrap and Turn, page 139)
sandwiched between 3 full rounds (described in
Steps 1 and 2). Each time you work Steps 1 and
2, you add about ¼" (6mm) in height to the
back. By repeating Steps 1 and 2, you can add
as many inches as you like.
3. To adjust the length of the legs, slip the leg
stitches to waste yarn and try on the shorts to
determine how many more inches to work.
Return stitches to the needle, and work as many
rows as desired until the beginning of the
inseam shaping.

Leg (Make 2)

With shorter needles, cast on 88 (94, 104, 115,
121) stitches loosely. Place marker, and join for
working in the round, being careful not to twist
stitches.

Work in stockinette stitch for ¾" (2cm). Purl 1
round to create a turning ridge. Work in
stockinette stitch for 2" (5cm) or the desired
length from the cast-on edge (see
customization instructions in Notes).

Slip all stitches to a stitch holder.

Join Legs

Slip the next 12 (13, 14, 15, 16) stitches from
the second leg onto a stitch holder, and slip all
but 12 (14, 16, 18, 20) stitches from the first Leg
onto the needles. The stitches on holders will
be joined later as the leg join using Three-
Needle Bind-off.

Hold Legs together at the inseam stitches, with
right sides facing. With longer needles, knit
stitches from both Legs and join for working in
the round—152 (162, 180, 200, 210) stitches.

Divide stitches, and place stitch markers at the
sides of hips so that 64 (70, 78, 86, 92) stitches
are in the front and 88 (92, 102, 114, 118)
stitches are in the back. Use different colored
stitch markers to designate the first marker as
Marker 1 and the second as Marker 2.

Short Row Shaping

Short rows (page 139) are worked across the
back stitches in stockinette stitch between
Markers 1 and 2. The front stitches wait on the
needle while short rows are worked, then all hip
stitches are worked in the round for 3 rounds in
between each set of short rows.

Step 1: Knit to 1 stitch before Marker 2. Wrap
and turn (page 139), and purl back to 1 stitch
before Marker 1. Wrap and turn.

Step 2: Return to working in the round across
the back stitches (the stitches between Markers
1 and 2) and continue around entire hip
circumference, picking up the wraps and
working them together with the stitches they
wrap as you pass them (page 139). Work 2
more rounds in stockinette stitch, ending at
Marker 1.

Repeat Steps 1 and 2, each time working to 2

stitches before the previous wrapped stitch, until 8 stitches have been wrapped at each side.

Work even in stockinette stitch until the back measures 6¾ (7¼, 7¾, 8¼, 8¾)" (17 [18.5, 19.5, 21, 22]cm) from the leg join.

Waistband

Create Eyelet Holes
Next Round Knit 88 (92, 102, 114, 118) Back stitches between Markers 1 and 2, k29 (32, 36, 40, 43), k2tog, yo, k2, yo, ssk, k29 (32, 36, 40, 43)—152 (162, 180, 200, 210) stitches.

Work even in stockinette stitch for ¾" (2cm). Purl 1 round to create a turning ridge. Work in stockinette stitch for 1¾" (4.5cm) from turning ridge. Bind off loosely.

Finishing

Fold up cuffs at turning ridge and whipstitch bound-off edge to wrong side of Leg.

Fold the waistband to the wrong side of the garment at the turning ridge. Using a yarn needle and matching yarn, whipstitch the bound-off edge to the wrong side, leaving an opening large enough to insert the waistband elastic; do not break yarn.

Cut the elastic 1" (2.5cm) longer than your waist measurement. Feed the elastic through the casing, pulling out both ends. Overlap the elastic ends by 1" (2.5cm), and sew them together with a sewing needle and thread. Slide the elastic back into the casing, and sew the casing closed with the yarn needle and yarn. Thread the ribbon length through the eyelet holes of the waistband.

Three-Needle Bind-off
With wrong side facing, pick up and knit 1 stitch from the body of the garment, slip 12 (13, 14, 15, 16) stitches from 1 leg join stitch holder onto the needle, pick up and knit 1 stitch from body of garment—14 (15, 16, 17, 18) stitches.

Repeat for the second set of leg join stitches, picking up and knitting 1 stitch from the garment at the beginning, slipping stitches onto a second needle, and knitting 1 stitch from the garment at the end. Hold the pieces with right sides facing, and using a third needle, knit together 1 stitch each from front and back needles. Repeat, then bind off the first stitch. Continue to bind off all the leg join stitches in this manner.

Weave in ends. Hand wash or machine wash with cool water on gentle cycle. Wring and blot to remove excess water, and dry flat.

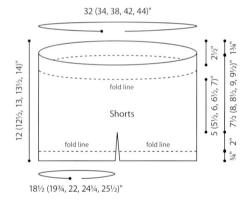

32 (34, 38, 42, 44)"

2½"

1¾"

fold line

12 (12½, 13, 13½, 14)"

5 (5½, 6, 6½, 7)"

7½ (8, 8½, 9, 9½)"

Shorts

fold line

fold line

¾" 2"

18½ (19¾, 22, 24¼, 25½)"

halter top

Skill Level

Easy

Sizes

XS (S, M, L, XL)

Finished Measurements

Bust Circumference: 23½ (25¼, 30¼, 35¼, 38)" (59.5 [64, 77, 89.5, 96.5]cm)
Length (from cast-on edge to top of neck): 19¼ (19½, 20¼, 21, 21½)" (49 [49.5, 51.5, 53.5, 54.5]cm)

Yarn

▧ 5 (5, 6, 6, 7) balls of Crystal Palace Yarns Bamboozle, 55% bamboo, 24% cotton, 21% elastic nylon, 1¾ oz (50g), 90 yd (82m), #0406 Carib Blue, ④ medium

Needles and Notions

▧ US size 8 (5mm) circular needle, 24" (60cm) long, or size needed to obtain gauge
▧ US size F-5 (3.75mm) crochet hook
▧ Stitch markers
▧ Yarn needle
▧ Metal ring, 1¼" (3cm) inside diameter

Gauge

19 stitches and 28 rounds = 4" (10cm) in stockinette stitch when worked in the round. Adjust needle size as necessary to obtain correct gauge.

Notes

1. The Halter Top is worked in the round from the lower edge to the underarm.

Designed to match the Tiny Shorts, this top is a quick knit that features the same unbelievably stretchy bamboo-cotton blend yarn. It's just a super easy tube knit in the round with a bit of simple shaping at the neckline. Work up this project in a couple of days, then add the cool silver ring and easy braided tie for a bit of sophisticated style.

Stitches are then bound off for the Back. The remaining Front stitches are worked back and forth in rows.
2. When binding off stitches, bind off in pattern. Slip the first stitch in each set of bound-off stitches to give a nice finished edge.

Make the Halter Top in the same color to match the Tiny Shorts (page 91) for a perfect casual outfit. Or, wear the Halter Top with capris, shorts, a skirt, or jeans.

Body

Cast on 112 (120, 144, 168, 180) stitches. Place marker, and join for working in the round, being careful not to twist stitches. Work 8 rounds in k2, p2 rib.

Change to stockinette stitch, and work until piece measures 15" (38cm) from the cast-on edge.

Divide for Front and Back

Bind off 57 (61, 73, 83, 89) stitches for Back, work to end of round—55 (59, 71, 85, 91) stitches.

Working back and forth in rows on the remaining 55 (59, 71, 85, 91) Front stitches, bind off 3 stitches at the beginning of the next 2 (2, 4, 6, 6) rows—49 (53, 59, 67, 73) stitches.

Bind off 2 stitches at the beginning of the next 4 (4, 6, 6, 6) rows—41 (45, 47, 55, 61) stitches.

Row 1 (RS) K2tog, knit to last 2 stitches, k2tog.
Row 2 P2tog, purl to last 2 stitches, p2tog.

Repeat these 2 rows 7 (8, 9, 11, 12) more times—9 (9, 7, 7, 9) stitches.

Repeat the first row 1 (1, 0, 0, 1) time(s) more—7 stitches remain.

Tab

Work even in stockinette stitch for 1" (2.5cm). Bind off.

Finishing

With right side facing, join yarn and single crochet evenly around the top edges.

Weave in ends. Hand wash or machine wash with cool water on gentle cycle. Wring and blot to remove excess water, and dry flat.

Fold top tab down over metal ring, and sew in place.

Braid 3 strands of yarn to make a neck strap approximately 30" (76cm) long. Fold strap in half. Slip folded end around the metal ring to make a loop. Pull ends through the loop to tighten.

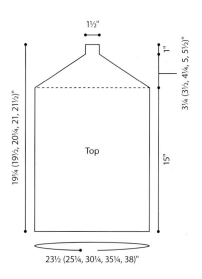

1½"

1"

3¼ (3½, 3½, 4¼, 5, 5½)"

19¼ (19½, 20¼, 21, 21½)"

Top

15"

23½ (25¼, 30¼, 35¼, 38)"

diva bikini

Skill Level

Intermediate

Sizes

XS (S, M, L, XL)

Finished Measurements

Bust Circumference (Top): 30 (32, 34, 36, 39)" (76 [81, 86, 91, 99]cm)
Hip Circumference (Bottom): 27 (28½, 32½, 36½, 39)" (68.5 [72.5, 82.5, 93, 99]cm)

Yarn

▤ 3 (4, 4, 5, 5) skeins Elle Stretch DK, 90% acrylic, 10% stretch polyester, 1¾ oz (50g), 170 yd (155m), #017 Black, **③** light

Needles and Notions

▤ US size 3 (3.25mm) knitting needles, or size needed to obtain gauge
▤ US size 3 (3.25mm) double-pointed knitting needles, or size needed to obtain gauge
▤ or US size 3 (3.25mm) circular needle, 40" (100.5cm) long, or size needed to obtain gauge
▤ US size D-3 (3.25mm) crochet hook
▤ Yarn needle
▤ 2 yd (2m) elastic thread (beading cord works), 3mm, black
▤ 3 Sunbelt Fashion plastic rings, 3mm, black

Lining Notions (Optional)

½ yd (0.5m) swimsuit lining fabric
1 pair Sew Sassy Swim Cup Inserts in appropriate size

More revealing than the Tankini (page 87), this swimsuit features the same great yarn that gives maximum versatility and stretch. Swarovski® flat-back crystals spell the word *diva* on the bottom for a totally hot custom look. Add sturdy plastic rings (with optional heart charms) to the top and bottom, and you've got bling that's beach-worthy.

Embellishment Notions (Optional)

2 heart-with-cutout charms, pewter
1 Jump ring, 10.9mm, stainless steel
42 Swarovski® Flat Back Crystals, 3.9mm SS16, Crystal AB
Aleene's® Jewel-It® Embellishing Glue
Chain-nose pliers
Sewing needle and thread

Gauge

28 stitches and 38 rows = 4" (10cm) in stockinette stitch. Adjust needle size as necessary to obtain correct gauge.

Notes

1. The Diva Bikini is worked back and forth in rows. The neck strap is worked in the round on double-pointed needles or a long circular needle (page 138 for Magic Loop).
2. The Bottom is worked in 1 piece from the front to the back.

Abbreviation

Sssk: Slip 3 stitches, 1 at a time, knitwise; insert left-hand needle into the front of all 3 slipped stitches, and knit them together.

top

Left Cup

Cast on 52 (56, 60, 64, 68) stitches. Purl 19 (21, 23, 25, 27), place marker, purl to end.

Shape Left Cup

Row 1 (RS) Knit to marker, M1, slip marker, k1, M1, knit to last 4 stitches, k2tog, k2.
Rows 2–4 Work even in stockinette stitch.

Repeat these 4 rows 3 (3, 4, 5, 6) more times—56 (60, 65, 70, 75) stitches.

Row 1 (RS) Knit to last 4 stitches, k2tog, k2.
Rows 2–4 Work even in stockinette stitch.

Repeat these 4 rows 3 (3, 2, 3, 2) more times—52 (56, 62, 66, 72) stitches.

Shape Left Top

Row 1 (RS) K2, ssk, knit to last 4 stitches, k2tog, k2.
Row 2 Purl.

Repeat these 2 rows 20 (22, 25, 27, 30) more times—10 stitches.

Work even in stockinette stitch for 2½" (6.5cm).

Shape Left Strap

Decrease 1 stitch at the beginning of the next 2 rows—8 stitches.

If you aren't already working on circular needles, slip the 8 stitches to double-pointed needles or a long circular needle, and cast on 8 stitches. Join for working in the round—16 stitches total. Work even in stockinette stitch for 10 (10, 10½, 10½, 11)" (25.5 [25.5, 26.5, 26.5, 28]cm).

Mitered Left End

Round 1 Ssk, knit to last 2 stitches, k2tog.

Repeat this round 6 more times—2 stitches. K2tog, break yarn, and pull the yarn end through the last stitch.

Right Cup

Cast on 52 (56, 60, 64, 68) stitches. Purl 33 (35, 37, 39, 41), place marker, purl to end.

Shape Right Cup

Row 1 (RS) K2, ssk, knit to marker, M1, slip marker, k1, M1, knit to end.
Rows 2–4 Work even in stockinette stitch.

Repeat these 4 rows 3 (3, 4, 5, 6) more times—56 (60, 65, 70, 75) stitches.

Row 1 (RS) K2, ssk, knit to end.
Rows 2–4 Work even in stockinette stitch.

Repeat these 4 rows 3 (3, 2, 3, 2) more times—52 (56, 62, 66, 72) stitches.

Shape Right Top

Row 1 (RS) K2, ssk, knit to last 4 stitches, k2tog, k2.
Row 2 Purl.

Repeat these 2 rows 20 (22, 25, 27, 30) more times—10 stitches remain. Work even in stockinette stitch for 2½" (6.5cm).

it girl style secret

Glam up this suit with a chic cover-up and sophisticated sandals when you wear it poolside. Or, throw on flip-flops and a pair of cut-off shorts for a laid-back sporty look. Swimsuit bra cup inserts give a sleek store-bought look to knitted bikini tops. Simply follow the super simple sewing instructions for inserting the optional cups and liner in your Diva Bikini top.

Decrease 1 stitch at the beginning of the next 2 rows—8 stitches.

If you aren't already working on circular needles, slip the 8 stitches to double-pointed needles or a long circular, and cast on 8 stitches. Join for working in the round—16 stitches. Work even in stockinette stitch for 10 (10, 10½, 10½, 11)" (25.5 [25.5, 26.5, 26.5, 28]cm).

Mitered Right End

Round 1 Ssk, knit to last 2 stitches, k2tog.

Repeat this round 6 more times—2 stitches. K2tog, break yarn, and pull the yarn end through the last stitch.

Ties (Make 2)

Cast on 3 stitches, using double-pointed needles.

I-Cord *Slide stitches to other end of needle and knit them, pulling yarn tightly across the back of the work. Do not turn work. Repeat from * to end to make an I-cord 15" (38cm) long, or desired length.

Join I-Cord to Bottom of Cup

With right side facing, *knit across the 3 stitches on needle and pick up 1 stitch along the bottom of one cup. Slide stitches to other end of needle and knit 2 stitches, ssk. Repeat from * to end across the bottom of the cup. Bind off.

Repeat to make a Tie across the second cup.

bottom

Front

Cast on 66 (74, 88, 102, 108) stitches. Work in stockinette stitch for 2" (5cm), ending with a wrong-side row.

Bind off 10 (10, 12, 14, 14) stitches at the beginning of the next 2 rows—46 (54, 64, 74, 80) stitches.

Row 1 (RS) K1, sssk, knit to last 4 stitches, k3tog, k1.
Row 2 Purl.

Repeat these 2 rows 2 (3, 4, 5, 6) more times— 34 (38, 44, 50, 52) stitches.

Row 1 (RS) K1, ssk, knit to last 3 stitches, k2tog, k1.
Row 2 Purl.

Repeat these 2 rows 5 (7, 9, 11, 11) more times—22 (22, 24, 26, 28) stitches. Work even in stockinette stitch until piece measures 8 (8, 9, 10, 11)" (20.5 [20.5, 23, 25.5, 28]cm) from beginning, ending with a wrong-side row.

Back

Row 1 (RS) K1, M1, knit to last stitch, M1, k1.
Row 2 Purl.

Repeat these 2 rows 20 (23, 27, 32, 35) more times—64 (70, 80, 92, 100) stitches.

Row 1 (RS) K1, M1, knit to last stitch, M1, k1.

Rows 2–4 Work even in stockinette stitch.

Repeat these 4 rows 4 more times—74 (80, 90, 102, 110) stitches.

Cast on 3 stitches at the end of the next 2 rows—80 (86, 96, 108, 116) stitches total.

Cast on 7 (7, 9, 10, 10) stitches at the end of the next 2 rows—94 (100, 114, 128, 136) stitches total.

Work even in stockinette stitch for 2" (32cm). Bind off.

Finishing

Top

With right side facing, join yarn and single crochet evenly around the cups. Thread elastic cord through the crochet edging.

Thread elastic cord through the I-cord under the cups, secure at the center of each cup, and try on the top to determine fit. For each cup, pull the cord to achieve proper snugness and fit, then secure with a stitch on the outside edge of the cup.

With the wrong side facing, place a plastic ring between the 2 cups, fold the inside corners of the cups over the ring, and pin in place. Try on the Top to get the right fit and coverage, and tack the ring in place with a sewing needle and thread.

Bottom

With right side facing, join yarn at hip opening, and single crochet around the top edge of the Bottom.

Weave elastic cord in and out of the crochet trim and around leg openings, if necessary, to achieve a comfortable fit.

At each side of Bottom, fold Front and Back edges around a plastic ring, and pin in place. Try on to get the right fit, and tack the rings in place with a sewing needle and thread.

Weave in ends. Machine wash in cool water on gentle cycle. Wring and blot to remove excess water, and dry flat.

Lining and Swim Cup Inserts (Optional)

Cut lining fabric to the shape of the swim cups plus ½" (13mm) seam allowance. Fold over ½" (13mm) seam allowance, and using a sewing needle and thread, tack lining into bathing suit, laying the edges of the swim cups flat as you go.

Try on Top, and pin the swim cup inserts into place. Tack inserts into bathing suit between the fabric and the lining..

Charm Embellishment (Optional)

With chain-nose pliers, open the jump ring, and slide on the pewter heart. Slide the jump ring onto the plastic ring on the Top. between the cups, and close the jump ring around the plastic ring. Repeat for the charm on Bottom.

Crystal Embellishment (Optional)

Following instructions on the Attaching Crystals sidebar, place crystals on the Bottom, beginning 4½" (11.5cm) from left ring and ¾" (2cm) from top edge of bottoms. For crystal placement, refer to the DIVA template (page 103).

attaching crystals

1. Place the crystals according to the template, or arrange them freehand.

2. Carefully align each to make them line up precisely; stand back frequently to check for any stones out of line.

3. One by one, lift each crystal with tweezers and place a tiny dab of permanent fabric glue on the back. Glue all crystals in place.

4. Set aside the Bottom, and allow it to dry overnight.

5. Heat cure the fabric to permanently affix your crystals. Preheat an oven to 350°F (176°C). Turn off the heat, and put the fabric in the warm oven for 30 minutes. Remove, and allow to cool.

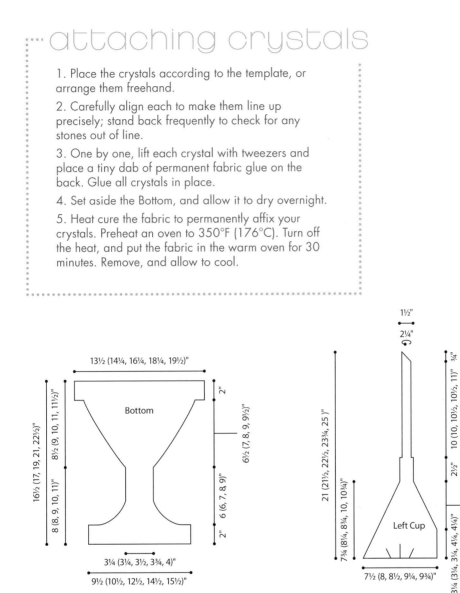

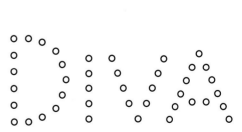

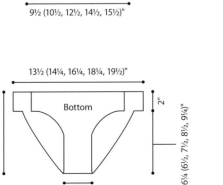

beaded wrap skirt

Skill Level

Intermediate

Size

One size

Finished Measurements

Width (excluding ties): 34" (86cm) Length (excluding fringe): 16" (40.5cm)

Yarn

▦ 2 skeins Bernat Cool Crochet, 70% cotton, 30% nylon, 1¾ oz (50g), 200 yd (182m), #74005 Crisp White, (**3**) light

Needles and Notions

▦ US size 13 (9mm) circular needle, 24" (61cm) long, or size needed to obtain gauge
▦ US size E-4 (3.5mm) crochet hook
▦ US size J-10 (6mm) crochet hook
▦ 12" (30.5cm) square of cardboard
▦ Yarn needle
▦ Medium steel beading needle
▦ 1 40g package each Transparent Seed Beads, #6, Light Turquoise Blue and Aqua
▦ 1 40g package each Rainbow Transparent Seed Beads, #6, Emerald Green and Teal
▦ 1 40g package Silver-Lined Round Hole Seed Beads, #6, Silver
▦ Aleene's® Fabric Fusion™ Permanent Dry Cleanable Fabric Adhesive™

Gauge

10 stitches and 16 rows = 4" (10cm) in Lace Pattern when worked flat.

This skirt is made with a soft cotton-blend yarn on big needles. It features an easy lace stitch and I-cord ties, with added fun for the crafty beader, too. The really spectacular element of this project is the fringe along the bottom edge of the skirt, which is embellished with hundreds of colorful beads. An ocean colorway dances along the ends of the fringe as you walk, its blues and greens sparkling in the summer sun.

Adjust needle size as necessary to obtain correct gauge.

Abbreviation

K1f&b: Knit into the front of the next stitch as usual, but leave that stitch on the left-hand needle and knit into the back loop of the same stitch. Then, slide the stitch off of the left-hand needle—1 stitch increased.

Notes

Lace Pattern K1, *yo, k2tog; repeat from * to end. Repeat this row to desired length.

Skirt

Cast on 17 stitches. Knit 1 row.

Increase Row Knit into the front loop and leave that stitch on the left-hand needle, knit into the back loop and leave that stitch on the left-hand needle, then knit into the front loop again and slide the stitch off of the left-hand needle (2 stitches increased), *yo, k2tog; repeat from * to end—19 stitches.

Repeat increase row 27 more times—73 stitches.

Row 1 K1f&b, *yo, k2tog; repeat from * to end—74 stitches.

Row 2 K1f&b, *yo, k2tog; repeat from * to last stitch, k1—75 stitches.

Row 3 K1f&b, k1, *yo, k2tog; repeat from * to last stitch, k1—76 stitches.

Row 4 K1f&b, k1, *yo, k2tog; repeat from * to end—77 stitches.

Rows 5–12 Repeat rows 1–4—85 stitches.

Work even in Lace Pattern until piece measures 16" (40.5cm) from beginning. Bind off very loosely. (If necessary, use a knitting needle a few sizes larger to keep the bind-off loose.)

Finishing

At 1 end of bound-off edge, pick up and knit 3 stitches close together.

I-Cord *Slide stitches to other end of needle and knit them, pulling yarn tightly across the back of the work. Do not turn work. Repeat from * to end until I-cord is 7" (18cm). Bind off. Make a second I-cord at the other end of bound-off edge.

With larger crochet hook and starting at the first I-cord, work 257 single crochets evenly spaced around the bottom edge of skirt, ending at the second I-cord.

Fringe

Cut a piece of cardboard, 12" (30.5cm) square. Wrap yarn around the cardboard 207 times. Cut the yarn at opposite ends of the cardboard piece to make 514 strands of yarn for fringe.

Insert smaller crochet hook under both loops of the first single crochet, fold 2 strands of fringe yarn in half over the hook, and pull the fringe yarn through the single crochet. Pull the ends of fringe yarn through the loop, and tug to tighten. Repeat to attach 2 fringe pieces into each single crochet.

Beads

String 3 beads on 2 of the 4 strands in each fringe group. On the first strand, thread a silver-lined, aqua, and light turquoise blue bead. On the second strand, thread a light turquoise blue, teal, and emerald green bead. Knot the ends of the strands to secure beads. Repeat for each fringe group.

Weave in ends. Secure any loose ends in place with Fabric Fusion™ or clear fabric glue. Hand wash in cool water. Wring and blot to remove excess water, and dry flat.

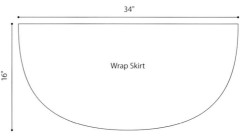

bead stringing

1. Pick up the first bead, and slide it onto the needle.
2. Continue as indicated in pattern until all beads are strung.

ocean waves poncho

Skill Level

Intermediate

Size

One size

Finished Measurements

Circumference (at hem, after finishing):
62" (157.5cm)
Length: 26" (66cm)

Yarn

▦ 3 skeins Bernat Cool Crochet, 70%
cotton, 30% nylon, 1¾ oz (50g),
200 yd (182m), #74130 Tie Dye
Shades, ③ light

Needles and Notions

▦ US size 13 (9mm) circular needle, 24"
(60cm) long, or size needed to obtain
gauge
▦ Yarn needle
▦ Aleene's® Fabric Fusion™ Permanent
Dry Cleanable Fabric Adhesive™
▦ 2 yd Satin ribbon, ¼" (6mm) wide,
blue

Gauge

10 stitches and 16 rows = 4" (10cm) in
Lace Pattern when worked flat. Adjust
needle size as necessary to obtain correct
gauge.

This poncho makes a dramatic statement
without being too precious or fussy. The lacy
lines work up quickly with a silky cotton-blend
yarn, big needles, and a super easy stitch that
you'll love. Really just a giant rectangle, this
garment is transformed by a pretty ribbon and
a bit of seaming into a work of art that will
make you look like a knitting genius.

Notes

Poncho is worked back and forth in rows, but a circular needle is used to accommodate the large number of stitches.

Lace Pattern K1, *yo, k2tog; repeat from * to last stitch, k1.

Repeat this row to desired length.

Poncho

Cast on 154 stitches. Work back and forth in garter stitch for 2" (5cm).

*Change to lace pattern and work for 4" (10cm).

Change to garter stitch and work for 2" (5cm).

Repeat from * to end until piece measures 26" (66cm) from beginning, ending with 2" (5cm) of garter stitch. Bind off loosely.

Finishing

Weave in ends. Dab Fabric Fusion™ or clear fabric glue on any ends that won't stay tucked in. Using a yarn needle and matching yarn, sew short edges of the rectangle together to form a tube.

Hand wash in cool water. Wring and blot to remove excess water, and dry flat.

Weave ribbon in and out of garter stitch section at the bound-off edge for tie. Tie ends together in a bow to gather the neck. Slip Poncho over your head, and adjust tie to suit.

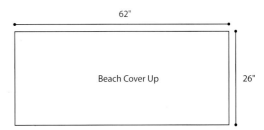

62"

Beach Cover Up

26"

it girl style secret

Wear the Ocean Waves Poncho beachside or poolside with the Diva Bikini (page 98) and flip-flops or strappy sandals, or wear it over a T-shirt and shorts all summer.

and
nights

Nights are all about going out, meeting up with friends, and having a great time. Your evenings are important, and whether yours involves a school formal, a party, a family night out, or a quiet dinner for two, you can make something unique and beautiful to wear. These glamorous projects include lovely embellishments that crafters of all levels can manage, and as always, the knitting is easy and quick.

gold halter top

Skill Level

Easy

Sizes

XS (S, M, L, XL)

Finished Measurements

Waist Circumference (unstretched): 16½ (18, 20¼, 22½, 23¾)" (42 [45.5, 51.5, 57, 60.5]cm)
Length: 17 (17, 17½, 18, 18)" (43 [43, 44.5, 45.5, 45.5]cm)

Yarn

- 3 (3, 4, 4, 4) skeins Patons Brilliant, 69% acrylic, 19% nylon, 12% polyester, 1¾ oz (50g), 166 yd (152m), #3023 Gold Glow, (3) light

Needles and Notions

- US size 5 (3.75mm) circular needle, 24" (60cm) long, or size needed to obtain gauge
- Stitch holders
- Stitch marker
- Yarn needle
- US size F-5 (3.75mm) crochet hook
- 2 Rivoli Rhinestone Buttons (M&J Trimming), 11mm diameter, Crystal AB/Gold

Gauge

36 stitches and 32 rounds = 4" (10cm) in k1, p1 rib (unstretched) when worked in the round. Adjust needle size as necessary to obtain correct gauge.

No tube worked in the round could be easier or more glamorous! This quick knit is full of couture details like crystal buttons to fasten the back of the collar, a very fitted look provided by the slimming 1 x 1 rib, and unbelievably easy shaping for a chic neckline. Follow the optional lengthening instructions to turn the halter into a tunic or a dress.

Notes

1. The Gold Halter Top is worked in the round from the lower edge to the underarm. Stitches are then bound off for the back. The remaining Front stitches are worked back and forth in rows.
2. To turn the top into a dress, slip stitches to a string and try on to determine how many more inches to work. Slip the stitches back to the needle, and work to the desired length before binding off stitches for the back at the underarm.

Body

Cast on 150 (162, 182, 202, 214) stitches. Place marker, and join for working in the round, being careful not to twist stitches. Work in k1, p1 rib for 9" (23cm) or desired length. Bind off 75 (81, 91, 101, 107) stitches (in rib pattern) for the back.

Front

Work back and forth on the 75 (81, 91, 101, 107) remaining stitches.

Rows 1–7 Work in k1, p1 rib.
Row 8 (RS) Ssk, work to last 2 stitches, k2tog.

Repeat these 8 rows 3 more times—67 (73, 83, 93, 99) stitches.

Rows 1–3 Work in k1, p1 rib.
Row 4 (RS) Ssk, work to last 2 stitches, k2tog.

Repeat these 4 rows 3 (3, 4, 5, 5) more times—59 (65, 73, 81, 87) stitches.

Divide for Neck
Next Row (RS) Ssk, work 17 stitches and leave unworked for left side of neck, work 21 (27, 35, 43, 49) stitches and place them on a stitch holder for center neck, work 17 stitches, k2tog. Turn work.

Right Neck

Row 1 (WS) Work in k1, p1 rib.
Row 2 Ssk, work to last 2 stitches, k2tog.

Repeat these 2 rows 7 more times until 2 stitches remain. P2tog, break yarn and pull yarn end through the remaining stitch to fasten off.

Left Neck

With wrong side facing, join yarn at neck edge to work Left Neck.

Row 1 (WS) Work in k1, p1 rib.
Row 2 Ssk, work to last 2 stitches, k2tog.

Repeat these 2 rows 7 more times until 2 stitches remain. P2tog, break yarn, and pull yarn end through the remaining stitch to fasten off.

Collar

Cast on 26 (26, 24, 22, 22) stitches, with right side facing, pick up and knit 9 stitches along Left Neck edge, work 21 (27, 35, 43, 49) stitches from center neck stitch holder in k1, p1 rib, pick up and knit 9 stitches along Right Neck edge, cast on 26 (26, 24, 22, 22) stitches—91 (97, 101, 105, 111) stitches.

Work 2 rows in k1, p1 rib, starting with a wrong-side row (purl the first stitch).

Buttonhole Row (WS) P1, k1, k2tog, yo, work in k1, p1 rib to end.

Work in k1, p1 rib until collar measures 2″ (5cm) from beginning, ending with a right-side row.

Repeat Buttonhole Row.

Work 2 rows in k1, p1 rib.

Bind off loosely in rib pattern.

Finishing

With right side facing, join yarn at collar edge of right Front, work single crochet evenly around edges of Front and back of body.

Weave in ends. Sew 2 buttons onto the Collar, opposite the buttonholes. Hand wash in cool water. Wring and blot to remove excess water, and dry flat.

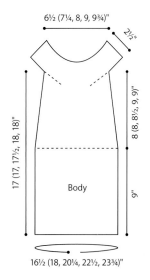

6½ (7¼, 8, 9, 9¾)″

2½″

8 (8, 8½, 9, 9)″

17 (17, 17½, 18, 18)″

9″

Body

16½ (18, 20¼, 22½, 23¾)″

it girl style secret

The Gold Halter Top matches the Gold Mini-skirt (page 117) perfectly to create a stunning ensemble. Or, wear the top with those jeans you love and a pair of ankle boots.

gold
mini-skirt

Skill Level

Easy

Sizes

XS (S, M, L, XL)

Finished Measurements

Waist Circumference (unstretched): 22½ (24½, 28½, 32½, 34½)" (57 [62, 72.5, 82.5, 87.5]cm)
Length: 16½ (16½, 17, 17½, 17½)" (42 [42, 43, 44.5, 44.5]cm)

Yarn

- 5 (5, 6, 7, 8) skeins Patons Brilliant, 69% acrylic, 19% nylon, 12% polyester, 1¾ oz (50g), 166 yd (152m), #3023 Gold Glow, (3) light

Needles and Notions

- US size 5 (3.75mm) circular needle, 32" (81cm) long, or size needed to obtain gauge
- US size 6 (4mm) circular needle, 32" (81cm) long
- US size 8 (5mm) circular needle, 32" (81cm) long
- Stitch marker
- Yarn needle
- 1 yd (91cm) elastic waistband, ½" (13mm) wide
- Sewing needle and thread

Gauge

36 stitches and 32 rounds = 4" (10cm) in k1, p1 rib (unstretched) when worked in the round on US size 5 (3.75mm) circular needle.

This skirt is designed to match the Gold Halter Top (page 113), and when worn together they substitute for a dress quite nicely. But you can also mix it up by pairing this skirt with a black sweater, a silky hot pink tank, or any other top with flair. The skirt's simple circular construction and flattering waistband create a sleek look that is easy to achieve for even the newest knitter. Make your skirt as long or short as you'd like with the optional instructions for a custom fit that flatters you.

Adjust needle size as necessary to obtain correct gauge.

Note

1. The Gold Miniskirt is worked in the round on circular needles.
2. The skirt is shaped by changing needle sizes. Stitches are cast on with the largest needle. Skirt is worked with the medium needle from the hem to the waist, and then the waist is worked on the smallest needle.
3. To adjust the skirt length, slip stitches to waste yarn and try on to determine how many more inches to work. Return stitches to the needle, and work as many rows as desired.

Skirt

With the largest needle, cast on 202 (220, 256, 292, 310) stitches. Place marker, and join for working in the round, being careful not to twist stitches.

Change to the medium needle, and work in k1, p1 rib for 5" (12.5cm) from beginning.

Change to the smallest needle, and work in k1, p1 rib until the piece measures 16½ (16½, 17, 17½, 17½)" (42 [42, 43, 44.5, 44.5]cm) or the desired length from the cast-on edge.

Shape Waistband

Purl 1 round to create a turning ridge.

Work even in k1, p1 rib for ¾" (2cm) from turning ridge. Bind off in rib.

Finishing

Fold the waistband to the wrong side of the garment at the turning ridge.

Using a yarn needle and matching yarn, whipstitch the bound-off edge to the wrong side, leaving an opening large enough to slide in the waistband elastic; do not break yarn. Cut the elastic 1" (2.5cm) longer than your waist measurement. Feed the elastic through the casing, pulling out both ends. Overlap the elastic ends by 1" (2.5cm), and sew them together with a sewing needle and thread. Slide the elastic back into the casing, and sew casing closed with the yarn needle and yarn.

Weave in ends. Hand wash in cool water. Wring and blot to remove excess water, and dry flat.

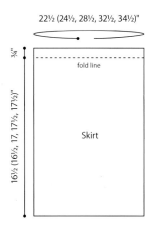

22½ (24½, 28½, 32½, 34½)"

¾"

fold line

16½ (16½, 17, 17½, 17½)"

Skirt

van gogh clutch

Skill Level

Easy

Size

One size

Finished Measurements

Width x Height (before felting): 20" (51cm) x 10½" (26.5cm), with an 8" (20.5cm) flap
Width x Height (after felting): 15" (38cm) x 7½" (19cm), with a 5½" (14cm) flap

Yarn

- ▪ 2 skeins Cascade 220, 100% Peruvian highland wool, 3½ oz (100g), 220 yd (201m), #8555 Black, **④** medium

Needles and Notions

- ▪ US size 10 (6mm) knitting needles, or size needed to obtain gauge
- ▪ Yarn needle
- ▪ 1 Sew-on snap, size 7

Embellishment Notions

- ▪ Dressmaker's chalk
- ▪ Tracing paper
- ▪ Aleene's Jewel-It Embellishing Glue
- ▪ Nymo Black Thread Bobbin nylon beading thread, size D
- ▪ 22 Swarovski® Crystal and Silver-Plated Brass Sew-On Montées, 6.4mm, SS30, Black Diamond
- ▪ 42 Swarovski Crystal and Silver-Plated Brass Sew-On Montées , 6.4mm, SS30, Light Topaz
- ▪ 47 Swarovski Crystal and Silver-Plated Brass Sew-On Montées, 6.4mm, SS30, Jet

Made from garter-stitch rectangles felted and embellished with glittering Swarovski crystals that swirl like the stars in Van Gogh's *Starry Night,* this beautiful bag is so simple to make. Fabulous crystals called montées encrust the purse, and their silver metal settings with special channels on the back make them super easy to sew on. The optional brocade lining is a snap to make and adds a classy touch.

- 47 Swarovski® Crystal and Silver-Plated Brass Sew-On Montées, 6.4mm, SS30, Topaz
- 43 Swarovski® Flat Back Rhinestones, 3.2mm, SS12, Crystal AB
- 3 Swarovski® Faceted Round Flat Back Sew-On Rhinestones, 10mm, Crystal

Lining Notions (Optional)

½ yard (0.5m) brocade fabric
Sewing needle and thread to match fabric

Gauge

15 stitches and 30 rows = 4" (10cm) in garter stitch when worked flat, before felting. Adjust needle size as necessary to obtain correct gauge.

Notes

1. The purse is worked back and forth in rows, then sewed together and felted.
2. Montées are glued on following a template, then sewed on to secure.

Back and Flap

Cast on 62 stitches.

Row 1 Knit.
Row 2 K1f&b, knit to last stitch, k1f&b.

Repeat these 2 rows 6 more times—76 stitches total.

Work even in garter stitch until piece measures 18½" (47cm) from beginning. Bind off.

Front

Cast on 62 stitches.

Row 1 Knit.
Row 2 K1f&b, knit to last stitch, k1f&b.

Repeat these 2 rows 6 more times—76 stitches.

Work even in garter stitch until piece measures 10½" (26.5cm) from beginning. Bind off.

Finishing

Sew Front to Back along the sides and bottom. Back piece will extend past the Front for the Flap.

Following instructions in the Felting sidebar (page 49), felt purse to finished measurements. When the purse has reached the correct size, remove it from the washer, and rinse it in cold water in the sink or tub until the water runs clear. Squeeze out excess water, and blot with clean, dry towels.

Stuff the bottom of the purse with plastic grocery bags to help it hold its shape while drying. Use as many bags as needed to make the bottom of the bag a bit rounded and full. Pin the sides and flap to a sheet of mat board, cardboard, or foam board to conform to the specified dimensions, and set aside the purse to dry.

Sew the snap onto the underside of Flap and the corresponding point on the front of the purse.

Crystal Embellishment

On a copy machine, enlarge the template (page 123) by 133%.

Lay tracing paper over the template, and trace the entire template with a black pen, leaving off the letters that indicate the crystal colors. Lay the tracing paper template onto a foam board or cardboard, and with a thick needle, poke holes into the center of each crystal icon. Lay the tracing paper template on the purse flap, centering the motif as shown in the photograph (page 120), and sprinkle crushed dressmaker's chalk across the paper, working the powder into each hole with your fingers or a soft brush. Remove the template.

Glue the crystals onto the purse flap, following white dots and referring to the original template for color placement.

Carefully align the crystals so they line up precisely; stand back frequently to ensure that no stones are placed incorrectly. Glue each crystal in place, one by one, lifting each crystal and placing a tiny dab of glue underneath to hold it in place. After all crystals are glued in place, allow the glue to dry overnight.

Flat-back crystals are permanently affixed to the purse flap, but the montées must also be sewn in place. Thread a sewing needle with Nymo thread, and sew each montée in place following the X-shaped channel on the bottom of each setting. Sew through the crystal's two channels, then move to the next closest crystal, never breaking the thread in between. The back of the purse flap will have little X's all over it. When you reach the end of your thread, tie a knot on the wrong side, and dab a bit of glue on it to secure it. Continue sewing until all montées are secured to the flap with thread. Do not rely on glue to hold the montées; it is only meant to hold the crystals in place while sewing. The montées must be sewn on, or they will pop off when you carry the clutch.

Lining (Optional)

From the brocade, cut 2 pieces to the same dimensions as the felted bag Front and Back sections, adding ½" (13mm) around each piece for a seam allowance and rounding the corners along the bottom edge. With right sides together, sew pieces together with a sewing needle and thread.

With wrong sides together, place the lining in the purse, and fold down and pin the top edge of lining to where you want it—a ½" (13mm) margin from the top edge of the purse looks very tidy. Press the fold line with a cool iron. Using a sewing needle and thread, topstitch ⅛" (3mm) from top edge to hold the lining in place.

To sew in the lining, turn the clutch inside out, and slip on the lining so that the right side is facing out. Pin the lining in place, measuring from the top edge of purse to make sure that the lining is evenly attached. Stitch along the top edge, very close to the seam at the top of the lining. Turn the clutch to the right side, and push the lining down inside. Tack the lining lightly along bottom to hold it down.

it girl style secret

Wear the Van Gogh Clutch with the Gold Mini-skirt (page 117) and the Gold Halter Top (page 113) for a sleek, classy look. Or, dress it down with jeans and a black turtleneck. Finish the clutch in style with the optional simple satin brocade lining.

montées

1. Apply a drop of permanent fabric glue to the project where you want to place the montée, following a template or freehand.
2. Place a montée on the glue. Continue adding drops of glue and montées until all the montées have been glued to the fabric according to the design.
3. Set aside for an hour to allow the glue to dry.
4. Thread a sewing needle with a double strand of beading thread, and knot the ends together.
5. Bring the needle up through the back of fabric, emerging beside an opening of a channel on the first montée.
6. Run the needle through the channel and back down into the fabric.
7. Cross across the back of the fabric to the opening of an opposite channel, and repeat.
8. Cross to the next closest montée, and repeat Steps 5–7.
9. Continue crossing to the next montée until all have been tacked through twice.
10. Ending on the wrong side of the fabric, knot ends, and cut thread.

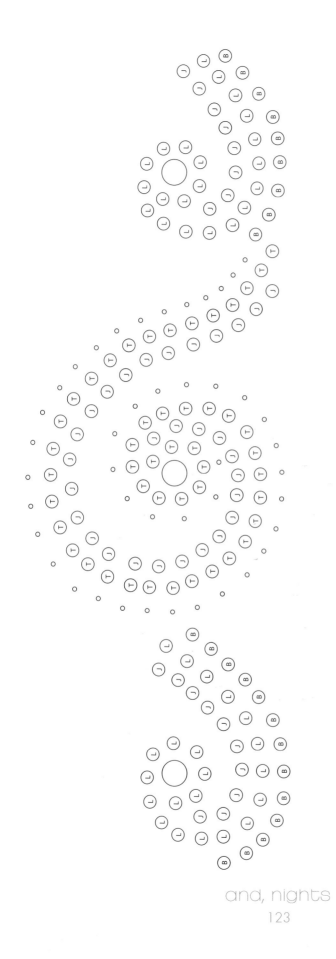

Color Key

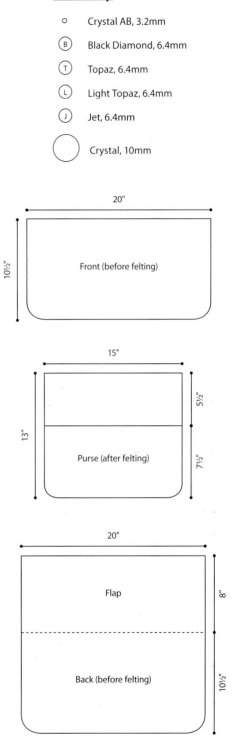

○	Crystal AB, 3.2mm
Ⓑ	Black Diamond, 6.4mm
Ⓣ	Topaz, 6.4mm
Ⓛ	Light Topaz, 6.4mm
Ⓙ	Jet, 6.4mm
⬤	Crystal, 10mm

20"

Front (before felting)

10½"

15"

5½"

13"

Purse (after felting)

7½"

20"

Flap

8"

Back (before felting)

10½"

sheath dress

Skill Level

Easy

Sizes

XS (S, M, L, XL)

Finished Measurements

Bust Circumference: 24½ (26½, 30½, 34½, 36½)" (62 [67.5, 77.5, 87.5, 92.5]cm)
Length from Underarm: 24½ (25, 26, 27, 27½)" (62 [63.5, 66, 68.5, 70]cm)

Yarn

■ 7 (7, 9, 10, 11) skeins Elle Stretch DK, 90% acrylic, 10% stretch polyester, 1¾ oz (50g), 170 yd (155m), #009 Robin Red, ③ light

Needles and Notions

■ US size 6 (4mm) circular needle, 24" (60cm) long, or size needed to obtain gauge
■ US size 6 (4mm) knitting needles, or size needed to obtain gauge (optional)
■ US size D-3 (3.25mm) crochet hook
■ Stitch marker
■ Stitch holder
■ Yarn needle
■ 1 yd (1m) elastic, ½" (13mm) wide
■ 1 yd (1m) elastic, ⅛" (3mm) wide
■ 1 swimsuit S hook, 1" (2.5cm) wide, clear plastic

Gauge

24 stitches and 32 rounds = 4" (10cm) in stockinette stitch when worked in the round. Adjust needle size as necessary to obtain correct gauge.

Totally hot, this project is just a giant stretchy tube with no shaping, seaming, or other tedious techniques to slow you down—and you can lengthen it with the optional instructions. The halter straps are super easy to knit, and a tidy single-crochet trim keeps them looking crisp and pretty. If you can knit a tube, you can knit this dress.

Notes

1. The Sheath Dress is worked on circular needles from the bottom up in the round to the armhole. It is then divided for the Front and Back, which are worked back and forth.
2. To adjust the length of the Sheath Dress, slip stitches to waste yarn and try on to determine how many more inches to work. Return stitches to the needle, and work as many rows as desired to the underarm.

Dress

With circular needles, cast on 148 (160, 184, 208, 220) stitches loosely. Place marker, and join for working in the round, being careful not to twist stitches.

Work in k2, p2 rib for ¾" (2cm).

Knit 1 row, purl 1 row.

Change to stockinette stitch, and work until piece measures 24½ (25, 26, 27, 27½)" (62 [63.5, 66, 68.5, 70]cm) or the desired length from the cast-on edge (see customization instructions in Notes, above).

Place next 74 (80, 92, 104, 110) stitches on a stitch holder for the Back.

Front

Work back and forth on the remaining 74 (80,
92, 104, 110) stitches for the Front.

Bind off 3 stitches at the beginning of the next
2 rows—68 (74, 86, 98, 104) stitches.

Shape Neckline
Row 1 (WS) P2tog, purl to last 2 stitches,
p2tog.
Row 2 K2tog, knit to last 2 stitches, k2tog.

Repeat these 2 rows 10 (10, 12, 13, 13) times
more—24 (30, 34, 42, 48) stitches. Bind off.

Back

With right side facing, slip the 74 (80, 95, 104,
110) stitches from the Back stitch holder to the
needle. Join yarn, and purl 1 row on the right
side for a turning ridge. Work in stockinette
stitch for ¾" (2cm). Bind off.

Finishing

Fold the Back casing to the wrong side of the
garment at the turning ridge. Using a yarn
needle and matching yarn, whipstitch the
bound-off edge to the wrong side, leaving both
ends open. Insert the wider (½"[13mm]) elastic,
and try on the dress. Pull elastic to fit across
Back, and pin in place. With sewing needle and
thread, sew both ends of elastic in place, and
cut off any excess elastic.

Using the pattern yarn, sew a casing for
elastic along the Front Neckline, using the

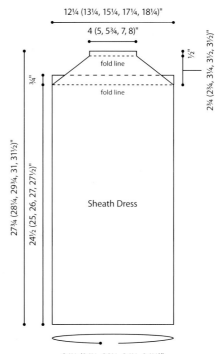

12¼ (13¼, 15¼, 17¼, 18¼)"

4 (5, 5¾, 7, 8)"

2¾ (2¾, 3¼, 3½, 3½)"

½"

fold line

¾"

fold line

27¾ (28¼, 29¾, 31, 31½)"

24½ (25, 26, 27, 27½)"

Sheath Dress

24½ (26½, 30½, 34½, 36½)"

herringbone technique to allow the elastic to move but not show on the front of the dress. Try on the dress, and pull the elastic to create the desired snugness for fit and support. Pin the ends of the Front elastic (½" [13mm] wide) to the ends of the Back elastic (½" [13mm] wide), and remove the dress. Sew the ends of elastic together with a sewing needle and matching thread.

Straps

Try on the dress again, and mark 1½" (3.8cm) on each edge for the placement of the Straps along bound-off edge of the Front.

With right side facing, pick up and knit 11 stitches where marked (optional straight needles may be used at this point).

Work in stockinette stitch for 3 rows.

Decrease Row (RS) K1, ssk, knit to last 3 stitches, k2tog, k1—9 stitches.

Work in stockinette stitch for 3 rows.

Repeat last 4 rows once more—7 stitches.

Continue to work in stockinette stitch until Strap measures about 10" (25.5cm) or desired length from the beginning. Bind off.

Repeat for second strap.

Fold 1½" (3.8cm) to the wrong side of the garment on 1 short end of the left Strap. Using a yarn needle and matching yarn, sew end in place. This is the casing for the hook.

Using a crochet hook, single crochet evenly around top edge of the Front, Back, and Straps.

Thread the short end of the right Strap through the hook, and fold the end to the wrong side of the garment. Using a yarn needle and matching yarn, sew end in place, securing the hook onto the right Strap.

Weave in ends. Machine wash in cool water. Wring and blot to remove excess water, and dry flat.

hand candy gloves

Skill Level

Intermediate

Sizes

S (M, L)

Finished Measurements

- Length from wrist to base of middle finger: 4 (4¾, 5½)" (10 [12, 14]cm)
- Wrist Circumference (excluding clasp): 5½ (6, 6½)" (14 [15, 16.5]cm)

Yarn

- 1 (1, 1) ball of J&P Coats® Metallic Knit-Cro-Sheen® Crochet Thread, Size 10, 86% mercerized cotton, 14% metallic, 100 yd (91m), Gold, (3) light
- or 1 (1, 1) ball of J&P Coats® Aunt Lydia's Classic Crochet Thread, Size 10, 100% mercerized cotton, 350 yd (320m), #401 Orchid Pink, (3) light

Needles and Notions

- Medium steel beading needle
- US size 5 (3.75mm) knitting needles, or size needed to obtain gauge
- US size D-3 (3.25mm) crochet hook
- Yarn needle
- Sewing needle and matching thread
- Aleene's® Fabric Fusion™ Permanent Dry Cleanable Fabric Adhesive™

For Gold Version

- 1 40g package each Silver-Lined Round Hole Seed Beads, #6, Root Beer and Gold
- 1 40g package Rainbow Transparent Seed Beads, #6, Amber
- Gold-Plated Sterling Silver Cloisonné Flat Round 3-Strand Clasp

These little gloves, knit in garter stitch, are like jewelry. Along the top of your hand, the gloves are studded with pretty beads; flip them over to admire a shiny silver or gold jewelry clasp on the strap—just like on a real bracelet. A Swarovski® crystal flower charm in a pretty setting dangles from the clasp.

For Pink Version

- 1 40g package each Ceylon Pastel Seed Beads, #6, white and pink
- 1 Filigree 16 x 14mm Tab Oval 2-Strand Box Clasp, silver plated
- 1 jump ring, 4mm, silver plated (optional)
- 1 jump ring, 6mm, silver plated (optional)
- Swarovski® Crystal AB 12 x 10mm Drop Charm, rhodium plated (optional)
- Chain-nose pliers (optional)

Gauge

24 stitches and 48 rows = 4" (10cm) in garter stitch when worked flat, with beads.
Adjust needle size as necessary to obtain correct gauge.

Notes

1. Count out about 50 of each color bead and place in separate plates or bowls, 1 bowl for each color. With a beading needle, string beads on yarn, alternating the colors as you go. See the Beading sidebar (page 22) for complete bead stringing instructions.

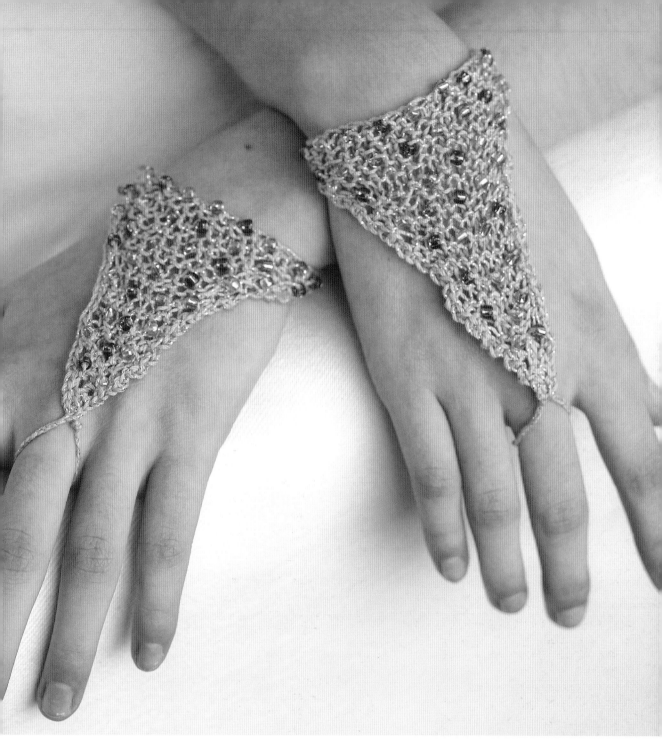

Wear the Hand Candy Gloves with anything. Try
the pink pair with the Capri Pants (page 57) and the
Lacy Camisole (page 74) for a casual look, or make
them glam in gold to match the Gold Halter Top (page
113)and the Gold Mini-skirt (page 107)—or dress up
the Sheath Dress (page 125).

2. The first ½" (13mm) after the cast-on row forms the wrist strap to which the clasps are attached. The height of the strap may be altered to accommodate a larger clasp. To add height, simply repeat Rows 2 and 3 as many times as necessary to match the height of the side of the clasp and to align the first and last jump rings with the first stitches on the first and last rows of the strap.

3. Optional charms can be added to your gloves with jump rings. Follow the Attaching Charms sidebar (page 130) for instructions.

Wrist Strap

Cast on 32 (36, 40) stitches, leaving a 12" (30.5cm) tail.
Row 1 Knit.
Row 2 Knit, slipping a bead into place every other stitch.
Row 3 Knit.

Hand

Row 4 Bind off 7 stitches, k18 (22, 26), bind off 7 stitches—18 (22, 26) stitches. (You will need to break the yarn, fasten off, and rejoin it for the next row.)
Row 5 Ssk, knit to last 2 stitches, k2tog—16 (20, 24) stitches.
Row 6 Knit, slipping a bead into place every other stitch.
Row 7 Ssk, knit to last 2 stitches, k2tog—14 (18, 22) stitches.
Row 8 Knit.
Rows 9 Ssk, knit to last 2 stitches, k2tog—12 (16, 20) stitches.
Row 10 Knit, slipping a bead into place every other stitch.
Row 11 Ssk, knit to last 2 stitches, k2tog—10 (14, 18) stitches.
Rows 12–13 Knit.
Row 14 Knit, slipping a bead into place every other stitch.
Row 15 Ssk, knit to last 2 stitches, k2tog—8 (12, 16) stitches.
Rows 16–17 Knit.

Row 18 Knit, slipping a bead into place every other stitch.
Rows 19–20 Knit.
Row 21 Ssk, knit to last 2 stitches, k2tog—6 (10, 14) stitches.
Row 22 Knit, slipping a bead into place every other stitch.
Rows 23–25 Knit.
Row 26 Knit, slipping a bead into place every other stitch.
Row 27 Ssk, knit to last 2 stitches, k2tog—4 (8, 12) stitches.
Rows 28–29 Knit.
Row 30 Knit, slipping a bead into place every other stitch.

Size Small Only
Row 31 Ssk, k2tog—2 stitches.
Row 32 Knit.

Sizes Medium and Large Only
Rows 31–32 Knit.
Row 33 Ssk, knit to last 2 stitches, k2tog—6 (10) stitches.
Row 34 Knit, slipping a bead into place every other stitch.
Rows 35–36 Knit.
Row 37 Ssk, knit to last 2 stitches, k2tog—4 (8) stitches.
Row 38 Knit, slipping a bead into place every other stitch.

Size Medium Only
Row 39 Ssk, k2tog—2 stitches.
Row 40 Knit.

Size Large Only
Rows 39–40 Knit.
Row 41 Ssk, knit to last 2 stitches, k2tog—6 stitches.
Row 42 Knit, slipping a bead into place every other stitch.
Rows 43–44 Knit.
Row 45 Ssk, knit to last 2 stitches, k2tog—4 stitches.
Row 46 Knit, slipping a bead into place every other stitch.
Row 47 Ssk, k2tog—2 stitches.
Row 48 Knit.

All Sizes
Bind off, leaving a 12" (30.5cm) tail.

Finishing

With right side facing, join the yarn at the edge of the strap and work single crochet evenly spaced down the edge of the glove to the first bound-off stitch. Fasten off, leaving a 12" (30.5cm) tail.

With right side facing, join the yarn at the last bound-off stitch, leaving a 12" (30.5cm) tail, and single crochet evenly along the opposite edge to the edge of strap. Fasten off.

Finger Ring

At the bound-off point of the glove are 3 yarn tails. Braid these 3 tails together tightly to measure 2½ (2¾, 3)" (6.5 [7, 7.5]cm) long, and tie a very loose knot. Try on the glove and loop the braided finger ring around your middle finger, holding or pinning the knot in place beside the beginning of the braid. Check the point of the glove from the front to make sure the braided finger ring makes a "V" centered at the point where it divides to encircle the finger. With a yarn needle, thread the remaining 3 ends through the last stitch on the wrong side at the point of the glove, pulling the knot snug against back of the glove. Try on the glove again to check the fit, and adjust the finger ring to suit. If necessary, retie the knot to achieve the perfect fit for the finger ring, and reaffix on the wrong side at the point of the glove beside the braided tails where they emerge from the glove. Weave in the ends, and use Fabric Fusion™ or clear fabric glue to secure the ends,

if desired. With 1 strand of pattern yarn, thread a sewing needle and tack the knot in place on the wrong side, ensuring that it doesn't show on the right side. A stitch or 2 may be needed to center the V at the top of the point.

Clasp

To attach the clasp, thread the yarn needle with the yarn tail and insert it through the jump ring on the clasp and back through the first stitch on the strap. Insert the needle into the second stitch, then the third stitch in the same row, weaving in and out from front to back to secure the tail further into the strap. Weave back through the same stitches and through the jump ring a second time. Insert the needle back into the strap, break the yarn, and weave in the end. Use Fabric Fusion™ or clear fabric glue to secure the yarn end and any other tails that may stick out or fray, hiding them on wrong side of the glove.

If desired, attach the optional charm to the clasp's jump ring as instructed below.

attaching charms

1. With chain-nose pliers, open the jump ring by twisting right side back, left side forward.
2. Slip the loop of the charm through the jump ring opening.
3. Slip the other jump ring or chain loop, or fabric loop, through the same opening in the jump ring.
4. With chain-nose pliers, close the ends of the jump ring by twisting right side forward, left side back.

lacy cap-sleeve bolero

Skill Level

Intermediate

Sizes

XS (S, M, L, XL)

Finished Measurements

Length: 13 (15, 16½, 18, 19½)" (33 [38, 42, 45.5, 49.5]cm)
Width from shoulder to shoulder: 17 (18, 20, 22, 23)" (43 [45.5, 51, 56, 58.5]cm)

Yarn

- 1 (1, 1, 1, 2) skeins Tilli Tomas Sequin Silk Disco Lights, 90% silk, 10% petite sequins, 3½ oz (100g), 225 yd (205m), Rattan, (4) medium

Needles and Notions

- US size 10.5 (6.5mm) circular needle, 24" (61cm) long, or size needed to obtain gauge
- US size 13 (9mm) circular needle, 24" (61cm) long
- Stitch marker
- Yarn needle

Gauge

10 stitches and 18 rows = 4" (10cm) in lace stitch on smaller needle when worked flat.
14 stitches and 24 rounds = 4" (10cm) in k2, p2 rib on smaller needle when worked in the round.

This bolero works up quickly in a luxurious silk yarn prestrung with tiny sequins. The lace stitch is super easy, so you can finish this garment in a couple of days. Perfect over little tops and dresses, the Lacy Cap-Sleeve Bolero is the ultimate accessory—simple yet stunning.

Adjust needle size as necessary to obtain correct gauge.

Notes

1. The Lacy Cap-Sleeve Bolero is a rectangle that is worked back and forth in rows on circular needles. It is worked from one sleeve edge to the other and then folded in half to make armholes.
2. Stitches are picked up along the long edges and worked in k2, p2 rib in the round for the neck and bottom edging.
Lace Pattern K1, *yo, k2tog; repeat from * to end. Repeat this row to desired length.

Bolero

With smaller needle, cast on 24 (28, 32, 36, 40) stitches loosely. Work 2 rows in k2, p2 rib, decreasing 1 stitch on second row—23 (27, 31, 35, 39) stitches.

Change to Lace Pattern, and work until piece measures 16½ (17½, 19½, 21½, 22½)" (42 [44.5, 49.5, 54.5, 57]cm) from the cast-on edge.

Work 2 rows in k2, p2 rib, increasing 1 stitch on first row—24 (28, 32, 36, 40) stitches. Bind off in rib.

Fold the lace rectangle in half lengthwise. Using a yarn needle and matching yarn, sew together 1" (2.5cm) at either end of long edges for armholes.

Edging

With right side facing and smaller needle, pick up and knit 108 (112, 128, 140, 148) stitches evenly around the remaining long edges of folded rectangle for neck and back edging.

Place marker, and join for working in the round, being careful not to twist stitches.

Work in k2, p2 rib for 2" (5cm). Work 1 round very loosely to prepare for switching to the larger needle (otherwise, the larger needle will not fit in the stitches). Change to the larger needle for the last round, and knit very loosely to make sure the last row will have some give. Bind off in loosely in rib.

Finishing

Weave in ends. Hand wash in cool water. Wring and blot to remove excess water, and dry flat.

Lace Section

17 (18, 20, 22, 23)"

9 (11, 12½, 14, 15½)"

17 (18, 20, 22, 23)"

6½ (7½, 8¼, 9, 9¾)"

Lace Section

Ribbing

1"   15 (16, 18, 20, 21)"   1"

4½ (5½, 6¼, 7, 7¾)"

2"

knitting guide

Here's a handy reference source for the abbreviations, techniques, and needle or crochet hook conversions needed to make the projects in this book.

Abbreviations

[ ] work instructions within brackets as many times as directed

( ) work instructions within parentheses in the place directed

* * repeat instruction following the double asterisks as directed

* repeat instruction following the single asterisk as directed

" inch(es)

BO bind off

cc contrasting color

cm centimeters

g gram

k knit

k1f&b knit 1 front and back

k2tog knit 2 stitches together

m meter(s)

M1 make 1 stitch

M1L make 1 stitch (left-leaning increase)

M1R make 1 stitch (right-leaning increase)

mm millimeter(s)

oz ounce(s)

p purl

p2tog purl 2 stitches together

psso pass slipped stitch over

p2sso pass 2 slipped stitches over

rep repeat(s)

RH right-hand

RS right side

sk2p slip 1, knit 2 together, pass sliped stitch over the knit 2 together—2 stitches decreased

sl slip

sl 1k slip 1 knitwise

sl 1p slip 1 purlwise

sl st slip stitch(es)

ssk slip, slip, knit these 2 stitches together—a decrease

sssk slip 3 stitches, knit these 3 stitches together—2 stitches decreased

sssp slip 3 stitches, purl these 3 stitches together—2 stitches decreased

st(s) stitch(es)

tbl through the back loop

tog together

WS wrong side

yd(s) yards

yo yarn over

general guidelines for yarn weights

The Craft Yarn Council of America has instituted a number system for knitting and crochet yarn gauges and recommended needle and hook sizes. The information provided below is intended as a guideline, and as always, swatching is key to being sure a chosen yarn is a good match for the intended project. More information can be found at www.yarnstandards.com.

CYCA	1	2	3	4	5
Yarn Weight	SUPER FINE Lace, Fingering, Sock	FINE Sport	LIGHT DK, Light Worsted	MEDIUM Worsted, Aran	BULKY Chunky
Avg. Knitted Gauge over 4" (10cm)	27–32 sts	23–26 sts	21–24 sts	16–20 sts	12–15 sts
Recommended Needle in US Size Range	1–3	3–5	5–7	7–9	9–11
Recommended Needle in Metric Size Range	2.25–3.25mm	3.25–3.75mm	3.75–4.5mm	4.5–5.5mm	5.5–8mm

special techniques and terms

circular knitting

Also known as knitting in the round (because you go around and around), circular knitting is the knitter's best friend! With circular knitting, knitting every row is transformed into stockinette stitch as if by magic. Using double-pointed needles (sets of 4 or 5 straight needles that are pointy at both ends) or circular needles (2 needle points connected by a cord or cable), you'll cast on stitches to 1 needle and join the stitches on the first round by slipping the tip of the right-hand needle under the first stitch on the left-hand needle and working that stitch with the yarn connected to the ball. Then, you'll just go around and around. Be careful not to twist stitches.

garter stitch

Knit every row when working back and forth in rows. Knit 1 round and purl 1 round when working circularly, in rounds.

gauge

Make a test swatch with pattern yarn by working a 6" x 6" (15cm x 15cm) square in the pattern stitch specified under "Gauge" in the instructions. Measure the number of stitches over 4" (10cm) with a ruler, laying the ruler in the center of the swatch. Measure the number of rows over 4" (10cm), too. These 2 numbers are your gauge, and it needs to match the instruction's gauge in order for your garment to come out right.

i-cord

*Slide stitches to other end of needle and knit them, pulling yarn tightly across the back of the work. Do not turn work. Repeat from * to end to make an I-cord to your desired length.

K2, p2 ribbing

Knit 2 stitches, purl 2 stitches—repeat across every row or round. On subsequent rows or rounds, knit the knit stitches and purl the purl stitches as they appear.

KIF&b

Knit into the front of the next stitch as usual, but leave that stitch on the left-hand needle and knit into the back loop of the same stitch. Then, slide the stitch off of the left-hand needle—1 stitch increased.

magic loop

The Magic Loop technique is a kind of circular knitting, worked on a circular needle that has a cable at least 32" long instead of a shorter circular needle or double-pointed needles. Cast on the desired number of stitches, divide them in half, and pull a length of cable out where they divide, sliding the yarn down to the tips of both needles. Hold the needles parallel to one another in front of you horizontally, with working yarn on the needle in back. Pull out the back needle, slipping the stitches onto the center of the cable (you now have 2 lengths of cable looping out in opposite directions). Bring the yarn around to the front needle, and knit the first half of stitches with the working yarn. Turn needles to continue knitting with working yarn coming from the back needle, pulling out the cable to maintain the 2-loop configuration at all times. Work across both needles to complete each round. For more detailed instructions, refer to *The Magic Loop* by Bev Galeskas.

MIL (left-leaning increase)

Find the horizontal bar between the last completed stitch on the right-hand needle and the next stitch on the left-hand needle. Insert the left-hand needle into the horizontal bar from back to front to pick it up onto the left-hand needle. Knit this new stitch through the front loop. Hint: If this method creates a hole, then you may have knit the raised bar through the back loop.

MIR (right-leaning increase)

Find the horizontal bar between the last completed stitch on the right-hand needle and the next stitch on the left-hand needle. Insert the left-hand needle into the horizontal bar from front to back to pick it up onto the left-hand needle. Knit this new stitch through the back loop. Hint: If this method creates a hole, then you may have knit the raised bar through the front loop.

place marker

Slip a safety pin, knitting marker, or a ring of colored yarn onto the needle to mark your place as directed in pattern.

provisional cast-on

Cast on with waste yarn, then join the pattern yarn after 1 or 2 rows. When you're ready to work the first row again (to add a ruffle or band of ribbing, for example), slide your needle through all those "live" stitches in the pattern yarn, and cut and remove the waste yarn. The waste yarn held your stitches for you so you don't have to pick up stitches from a bulky cast-on edge. Very easy, very clean.

short rows

Short rows are used in several patterns to add fullness to a piece of knitting (e.g., the back of pants or shorts) without adding length all around the project. Each short row is actually 2 partial rows (back and forth) sandwiched between full rows or rounds. Each short row adds height to the section in which the shaping occurs. By repeating short-row shaping, you can add—or eliminate—as much length as you like. To determine how many inches to add (or subtract), slip all of the stitches onto waste yarn, try on the project, and refer to the pattern for guidance on how much length each short row adds. See the Wrap and Turn entry for further instructions.

stockinette stitch

Knit on the right-side rows, purl on the wrong-side rows when working back and forth in rows. Knit all rounds when working circularly, in rounds.

wrap and turn

To wrap and turn a stitch when making short rows, do as follows: Bring the yarn to the front of your work, slip the next stitch purlwise from the left-hand needle to the right-hand needle, bring the yarn to the back of your work (to wrap the yarn around the slipped stitch), slip the slipped stitch purlwise back onto the left-hand needle, and turn your knitting to the other side (to work in the other direction, even though you are in the middle of a row). When you later come to work a wrapped stitch—on the next row or after you have finished your short rows—first pick up the wrap onto the left-hand needle, then work it together with the stitch that it resource guide

As you work on the projects, flip back to these pages to find out where to get supplies, yarn, and knitting or crafting help. You'll also find the templates to use as guides when applying crystals.

books

Many of the following titles live on the shelf in my studio and get used constantly. I couldn't run my business without the help of these authors. When you get stuck and don't know how to do a technique, one of these books surely can provide the information and advice you need. Borrow them through your local library, or buy them at your local bookstore or online.

At Knit's End—Stephanie Pearl-McPhee, Storey Publishing, 2005

The Beader's Companion—Judith Durant and Jean Campbell, Interweave Press, 2005

Big Book of Knitting—Katharina Buss, Sterling, 2001

Complete Beading for Beginners—Karen Rempel, Harbour, 1996

The Knitter's Book of Finishing Techniques—Nancie Wiseman, Martingale, 2002

The Knitter's Companion—Vicki Square, Interweave Press, 2006

Knitter's Handbook—Montse Stanley, Reader's Digest, 1999

Knitting from the Top—Barbara G. Walker, Schoolhouse Press, 1996

Knitting Rules!—Stephanie Pearl-McPhee, Storey Publishing, 2006

Knitting Without Tears—Elizabeth Zimmerman, Fireside, 1973

The Magic Loop—Bev Galeskas, Fiber Trends, 2002

Nicky Epstein's Beginner's Guide to Felting—Nicky Epstein, Leisure Arts, 2006

The Principles of Knitting—June Hemmons Hiatt, Simon & Schuster, 1989

Stitch N' Bitch—Debbie Stoller, Workman Publishing, 2004

yarn

The yarns chosen for this book were reviewed for specific qualities to ensure quality garments. Although you can substitute other yarns for those used in each pattern, many of the yarns in this book were selected because of special fiber combinations that make them perfect for their projects. Check out these companies online to find a listing of the stores nearest you that carry their yarns.

Berroco, Inc.
14 Elmdale Road
P.O. Box 367
Uxbridge, MA 01569
508–278–2527
www.berroco.com

Cascade Yarns
1224 Andover Park E
Tukwila, WA 98188
www.cascadeyarns.com

Straw into Gold, Inc.
Crystal Palace Yarns
160 23rd Street
Richmond, CA 94804
www.straw.com

Harrisville Designs
Center Village
P.O. Box 806
Harrisville, NH 03450
800–338–9415
www.harrisville.com

Needful Yarns
60 Industrial Parkway, PMB #233
Cheektowaga, NY 14227
416–398–5300
www.needfulyarnsinc.com

Spinrite—Patons and Bernat yarns
Box 40
Listowel, ON, N4W 3H3
Canada
1–800–265–2864
www.spinriteyarns.com
www.patonsyarns.com
www.bernat.com

South West Trading Company
866–794–1818
www.soysilk.com

Plymouth Yarn Company, Inc.
500 Lafayette Street
Bristol, PA 19007
215–788–0459
www.plymouthyarn.com

Tilli Tomas
72 Woodland Road
Jamaica Plain, MA 02130
617–524–3330
www.tillitomas.com

Unicorn Books and Crafts—Elle Stretch
1338 Ross Street
Petaluma, CA 94954
1–800–289–9276
www.unicornbooks.com

Nashua Handknits
Westminster Fibers, Inc.
4 Townsend Avenue, Unit 8
Nashua, NH 03063
800–445–9276
www.westminsterfibers.com

Needles and Notions

This is a very short list of my favorite supplies of needles and hooks. Visit their websites to find the store nearest you that sells these wonderful tools, or buy from online retailers.

Bella Blue—Hand painted knitting needles and crochet hooks.
P.O. Box 583
Mathews, VA 23109
www.bellablue.net

Denise Interchangeable Knitting Needles—My favorite circular needle kit containing all the needle sizes and the cable lengths you'll need to make the garments in this book, plus add-ons like 40" cables.
1618 Miller School Road
Charlottesville, VA 22903
888-831-8042
www.knitdenise.com

Widget Products, Inc.—Crochet Lite Hooks that come in yummy sherbet colors and light up when you use them.
11235 Davenport Street
Suite 109
Omaha, NE 68154
www.widgetproducts.net

Craft Supplies and Purse Hardware

I selected the best crafting materials available to use for the projects in this book. Because I personally tested each one before recommending it, you can be assured of the quality of these supplies.

Many of these popular supplies and materials should be available from your local craft store. Or, visit each company online to find out where you can buy their products. Some also sell directly to the public, so check them out.

Crazy Crow Trading Post—Rabbit Fur
1801 Airport Road
Pottsboro, TX 75076
1-800-786-6210
www.crazycrow.com

Duncan Enterprises—Aleene's glues
5673 East Shields Avenue
Fresno, CA 93727
800-438-6226
www.duncancrafts.com

FiberTrends, Inc.—Suede slipper soles
P.O. Box 7266
East Wenatchee, WA 98802-7266
www.fibertrends.com

Fire Mountain Gems and Beads—Beads, crystals, beading thread and wire, and clasps
1 Fire Mountain Way
Grants Pass, OR 97526-2373
800-423-2319
www.firemountaingems.com

M & J Trimming—Buttons, ribbons, and lace
www.mjtrim.com
1-800-9-mjtrim

Muench Yarns, Inc.—Grayson E. Leather Purse Handles
1323 Scott Street
Petaluma, CA 94954-1135
800-733-9276
www.muenchyarns.com

Sew Sassy Fabrics—Bra cups, lingerie notions, swim cups, and notions
Dept PB 727
504 Andrew Jackson Way
Huntsville, AL 35801
256-536-4405
www.sewsassy.com

Simple Shoemaking—"Soles with an Edge" outdoor soling for felted footwear
Sharon Raymond
145 Baker Road
Shutesbury, MA 01072
413-259-1748
www.simpleshoemaking.com

index

Page numbers in *italics* indicate photos and schematics.